Amsterdam
Architecture
City

T0284676

Paul Groenendijk, Peter de Winter
photography: Ossip van Duivenbode

nai010 publishers

Welcome in Amsterdam

Featuring the 100 best buildings – from the world-famous Rijksmuseum to the brand-new Sluishuis in IJburg – this guide presents a diverse overview of Amsterdam architecture through the ages. From the striking canal houses on the seventeenth-century ring of canals to the most recent architectural gems. With a wide variety of building types, from unknown architects to internationally acclaimed starchitects, in all kinds of construction methods and architectural styles. Amsterdam is most famous as a city of canals and historical monuments, but it is also the city of Berlage's Commodity Exchange, Duiker and Bijvoet's functionalist Open Air School, the expressionist housing of the Amsterdam School, Brutalist post-war reconstruction projects, 1970s urban renewal and eye-catching new buildings in the former port and industrial areas. But the city is more than just buildings. Therefore, we also focus on the parks and public green spaces and the best places to eat, drink and stay. With anecdotes, quotes, interesting facts and historical details about the buildings and their immediate surroundings at the bottom of the pages, which together paint an even richer picture of the dynamics and characteristics of this unique metropolis.

Contents

Stationsplein 9-33
P.J.H. Cuypers, A.L. van Gendt
1876-1889
L.J. Eijmer (constr.); J.F. Vermeylen,
G. Sturm, E. Gillet, E. Roskam, M.J.
Noppeney, M. Van Langendonck (art);
Benthem Crouwel (ren. 1996-2018)

Because of its prominent location on the IJ, the commission for the new Central Station was given to a famous architect, Pierre Cuypers (1827-1921), in 1876. The construction of Central Station also meant that there was no longer an open view of the waters of the IJ from the city's medieval centre. Cuypers designed the more than 300-metre-long brick building with its two characteristic towers next to the monumental entrance hall as a new gateway to Amsterdam. Like his almost simultaneously realized design for the Rijksmuseum **25**, the station building features a rich decoration programme both in its interior and on the outside. The top of the facade bears the coat of arms of the client, the State of the Netherlands, with the coat of arms of Amsterdam right below it. Cuypers collaborated on the design with Dolf van Gendt, who had experience with the railways as a structural engineer. The 45-metre-wide roof over the tracks, designed by civil engineer L.J. Eijmer, was installed in 1889 as the final part of the construction. The station has been updated with renewals and expansions since its construction. Most recent is the underground connection to the metro network **75** by Benthem Crouwel.

Rotterdam becomes Amsterdam

In the Cuyperspassage on the west side of the station, designer Irma Boom (1960) designed an impressive more than 100-metre-long mural with over 70,000 tiles. It is inspired by the eighteenth-century tile panel '*s Lands schip Rotterdam en de haringvloot (the Warship Rotterdam and the Herring Fleet)* from circa 1700 by Cornelis Boumeester. On the stern of the ship, Boom replaced the coat of arms of Rotterdam with the Amsterdam

coat of arms with the three St Andrew's crosses. The title of the work is also 'Amsterdammed': Boom calls it *Zeezicht aan het IJ (Seascape on the IJ)*.

2 Oosterdoks Island

Oosterdokskade
EEA i.c.w. various architects
2001-2007

The Oosterdoks Island, or ODE, next to the Central Station ❶ was completely taken up by a large PTT postal centre from the 1960s onwards. On the basis of an urban development plan by Erick van Egeraat (1956), following the demolition of this complex the site was filled with cultural and recreational functions in high building density: the 2007 public library (OBA) by Jo Coenen, the 2008 conservatory by

Frits van Dongen, a hotel, shops, restaurants, offices and housing. An office building for booking.com was added most recently in 2023, designed by UN Studio. Underneath the entire island is a loading and unloading area and a car park. The delivery road at the rear against the railway yard is overbuilt. A bicycle and pedestrian bridge connects the Oosterdok with Nemo ❹. According to the designers, the radial structure of the urban plan would represent a 'counterpoint to the ring of canals'.

Amsterdam, that great city...

Traditionally, all Amsterdam buildings were built on wooden piles because of the weak subsoil. These were driven deep into the peat layer until they reached the hard sand layer at a depth of 13 metres. For the Central Station ❶, for instance, 8,687 wooden piles were sunk in 1881. As many as 13,659 wooden piles were used in the construction of the Royal Palace on Dam Square ❾ in 1648, which were

imported from Norway especially for this purpose. There is also a well-known children's song:

Amsterdam, that great city, Which is built on piles;
If that city fell over one day, Who would be the one to pay?

Prins Hendrikkade 108-114
J.M. van der Meij
1912-1916
M. de Klerk, P.L. Kramer (ass.); J.G. van
Gendt, A.D.N. van Gendt (constr.); H.A.
van den Eijnde, H.L. Krop, W.C. Brouwer,
W. Bogtman, C.A. Lion Cachet, Th.W.
Nieuwenhuis, J.A. Rädecker (art); R.
Kentie (ren. 2005-2008)

The Shipping House was a joint office
building for six Amsterdam shipping
companies. Almost all pioneers of the
Amsterdam School were involved in
its construction, making the Shipping
House one of the pinnacles of this
architectural style. Architect Johan
Melchior van der Meij (1878-1949) was
brought in for the design. The relatively
inexperienced architect collaborated
with Michel de Klerk (1884-1923) and
Piet Kramer (1881-1961), whom he had
met at the office of Ed. Cuypers. The
brothers J.G. and A.D.N. van Gendt
were responsible for the construction
and practical design. Also because of
the involvement of a large number of
visual artists, great artistic freedom and ample
financial resources, the
result was a veritable
gesamtkunstwerk.
The specific location on
the sharp point of a building block is accentuated
by a higher corner build-
ing containing the main
entrance. On the floors
above the entrance were
the boardrooms of var-
ious shipping compan-
ies. The corner section
somewhat resembles the
bow of a ship. The use
of a concrete skeleton
meant that the walls had
no load-bearing func-
tion. The north facade
has twelve bays, the west
facade has fifteen; the
piers have lavish orna-
mental brickwork, statues of mate
and sailor, medallions and other decorative elements. All the ornaments
are based on shipping and the illus-
trious past of Dutch seafaring. A team
of sculptors led by Hendrik van den
Eijnde and Hildo Krop made the sculptures. Under the windows of the floor
where a particular shipping company
was housed, special custom decorations were added: Hercules for the
KNSM, two residents of Suriname in
a canoe for the KWIM, a scale for the
SMN, an anchor with lobster and ibex
for the KPM and a Buddha statue with
dragon and chrysanthemum for the
JCJL. Sculpted personifications of the
oceans can be found around the main
entrance. Wrought ironwork was used
on the gates, a display case in the
facade (for ship models) and for the
lettering. The tower is decorated with
lead representations of the four wind
directions.
The tall entrance hall and central
stairwell feature a glass canopy with
stained glass. Marble has been used
alongside plastered concrete walls.

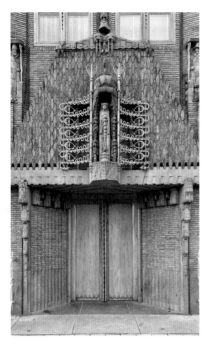

The geometrically decorated central stairwell is the spatial highlight. After the last shipping company left the building in 1981, it became the property of the municipality. Since 2008, it has been in use as a hotel.

Chet Baker

The Netherlands, and Amsterdam in particular, has always been a refuge where Protestants, Huguenots and freethinkers could find a place. Many musicians also sought freedom in Amsterdam for short or longer periods, including Nina Simone, Dusty Springfield, Arthur Conley, Kid Congo Powers and the jazz musicians Don Byas, Ben Webster and Chet Baker, who have all died here. Trumpet player and singer Chet Baker (1929-1988) came here mainly because of the liberal drug policy. He lived in a hotel at 53 Prins Hendrikkade, near the Zeedijk, where he could score heroin. There, on the night of 12-13 May 1988, he fell out of the window. A plaque by artist Roman Zhuk (1955) has been mounted in the facade in 1999.

Oosterdok 2
R. Piano
1990-1997

The Nemo Science museum is an interactive educational museum dedicated to science and technology. The building is situated at the head of the IJtunnel below, which was used as a foundation. At the spot where the traffic goes into the tunnel, Italian architect Renzo Piano (1937) has created a striking building that seems to rise out of the water like a ship. The ship-like character of the building is enhanced by the cladding with green oxidized copper wall panels. The ascending roof is publicly accessible and acts as a 22-metre-high urban plaza with impressive views over the city and maritime surroundings. The interior consists of a neutral open, continuous space with tiered floors incorporating public and exhibition functions.

Arcam

Prins Hendrikkade 600 has been home to Amsterdam's architecture centre Arcam since 2003. Architect René van Zuuk (1962) converted Renzo Piano's small viewing pavilion on this site into a compact and sculptural three-storey building. It is clad in coated aluminium that flows around the building in a continuous plane. Glass facades have been installed in the open spaces within this sculpted shape.

Kattenburgerplein 1
D. Stalpaert
1656-1657
Dok Architects (ren. 2006-2011),
Ney & Partners (roof)

Since 1973, the National Maritime Museum has been housed in the monumental 's Lands Zeemagazijn (National Sea Arsenal), built between 1656 and 1657 in a record time of one year by city architect Daniël Stalpaert (1615-1676) for the Admiralty of Amsterdam. The warehouse stored ship supplies and weapons for the war fleet. The robust square building was built in the style of Dutch classicism. Its austere appearance and location surrounded by water emphasized its warehouse function. After a fire in 1791, the walls were plastered and the building appears to be built of large blocks of sandstone. In a major renovation in 2011, the geometry of the building became the starting point for its new function as the Maritime Museum. The large courtyard was given a central public function and fitted with an impressive roof with a steel frame inspired by the compass lines on old sea charts.

Bridge keeper's houses 🛏

At least as special as the Amsterdam bridges are the tiny bridge keeper's houses. Twenty-eight of those bridge houses are in use today as hotel suites. From the 1673 Amstelschut bridge house by architect Joannes Hudde via several designs by bridge builder Pieter Lodewijk Kramer to the 2009 Haveneiland lock by Quist Wintermans. With 360-degree views over the harbour on the Kortjewants bridge (Dick Slebos, 1967).

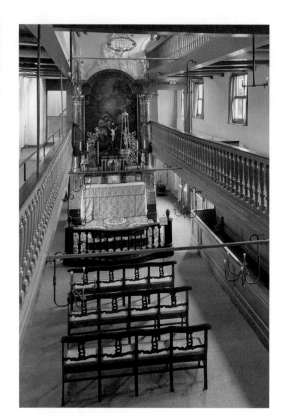

Oudezijds Voorburgwal 38-40
1630/1661
Architect unknown
Claus Van Wageningen (exp. 2008-2015)

Museum Ons' Lieve Heer op Solder (Our Lord in the Attic) is a former conventicle, housed in a traditional canal house from 1630. The property was bought in 1661 by Jan Hartman, a merchant of German origin, who immediately had it converted into a luxury residence with a range of living quarters, bedsteads, kitchens and an impressive, centrally located and classicist-style salon. In the attic of his home, the Roman Catholic Hartman realized a conventicle, which tolerant but Protestant Amsterdam at the time turned a blind eye to. The jewel of the attic church is the Baroque altar with a folding mahogany pulpit in the base of one of the marbled columns. With its double galleries across the long sides, the surprisingly high attic church accommodated about 150 churchgoers, who could reach the church via a side entrance in the alley. To the right of the alley, a new entrance building designed by Claus Van Wageningen was built in 2015, connecting the two properties via an underground passage.

Narrowest Facade

In the seventeenth century, taxes had to be paid in Amsterdam for the width of the facade. The narrowest facade in Amsterdam can be found at Singel 7, which is barely a metre wide. This is a rear facade, by the way. Amsterdam's narrowest house can be found at Oude Hoogstraat 22, which has a facade width of 2.02 metres. With a depth of five metres, it is also known as the smallest house in Amsterdam.

Sint Antoniesbreestraat and environs
Van Eyck & Bosch
1975-1983

The urban renewal of the Nieuwmarkt district took place after the neighbourhood was largely flattened in the 1970s for the construction of the metro. Under the slogan 'Building for the neighbourhood', local residents, activists and architects joined forces to renovate the neighbourhood with restoration of historical buildings, new construction adapted to the scale of the surroundings and priority to housing, with small-scale business and shops. The various new development projects show the typical 1970s conception of adapted new construction; small scale suggested by roof shapes and traditional brick construction. The architects Aldo van Eyck (1918-1999) and Theo Bosch (1940-1994) played an important role in the renewal of the Nieuwmarkt neighbourhood. One of their most important works is the Pentagon, a pentagonal, more or less closed building block at the head of Sint Antoniesbreestraat, which follows the existing building lines with 88 dwellings around a semi-public courtyard.

'Houses, not tubes'

The demolition of much of the Nieuwmarkt neighbourhood led to mass protests and triggered the heavy Nieuwmarkt riots on 24 March and 8 April 1975. The clash involved 800 police officers with water cannons, armoured cars, bulldozers, batons and tear gas. From the roofs of the buildings that were to be demolished, activists pelted the police with stones and household items. Dozens of people were injured. The Nieuwmarkt riots did not prevent the metro from being constructed, but it did get urban renewal on the political agenda.

8 City Hall and Music Theatre (Stopera) ☕ 🍴

Amstel 1-3
W. Holzbauer, C.G. Dam
1979-1987

The creation of a new city hall was an arduous and lengthy process. In 1936, there was a competition with 225 entries for a site on Frederiksplein square. The winners J.F. Berghoef and J.J.M. Vegter elaborated their plan after the war for a new location: Waterlooplein. In the early 1960s, this design was rejected and a new competition followed in 1967. From 804 entries, the proposal by Austrian architect Wilhelm Holzbauer (1930-2019) was chosen. This also threatened to fail due to political reluctance and high costs, as did a plan for an opera house by architects G.H.M. Holt and B. Bijvoet in Amsterdam-South. In 1979, the bright idea was conceived to combine the two projects: city hall and opera house were to become the Stopera. Holt's son-in-law Cees Dam (1932) worked out the plans with Holzbauer. Despite the usual storms of protest from the public and architects, the project went ahead. By building the L-shaped office section around the opera hall, space and costs were saved. There are foyers around the main hall; the curtain wall features marble-clad concrete screens.

The Docker

The monument De Dokwerker (The Docker) on Jonas Daniël Meijerplein was unveiled on 19 December 1952. The sturdy worker by sculptor Mari Andriessen (1897-1979) symbolizes the first major act of resistance by the Dutch population against the German occupiers: the February strike of 25 and 26 February 1941. It was prompted by the first pogroms in Amsterdam in which 427 Jewish men were taken hostage. The strike organized by the Communist Party of the Netherlands started in Amsterdam and quickly spread to surrounding municipalities, but was ruthlessly crushed by the Germans.

Dam/Nieuwezijds Voorburgwal 147
J. van Campen
1648-1665
J.W. Blaeu, F. Hemony, A. Quellijn (art)

The Royal Palace on Dam Square was originally built as the new city hall of Amsterdam. The enormous building, the magnum opus of architect Jacob van Campen (1596-1657), was meant to reflect the great power and wealth of Amsterdam in the seventeenth century. The monumental sandstone building was built in the style of Dutch classicism. The symmetrical facades are crowned with triangular pediments with marble sculptures representing Amsterdam's prosperity and dominance in the world's oceans. Astride the rear of the building is the six-metre-high bronze statue of Atlas, cast in 1664 by bellfounder François Hemony. At the centre of the building, between two courtyards surrounded by galleries, is the civic hall. An astronomical chart and maps of the eastern and western hemispheres were inlaid in the marble floor after the design of cartographer Joan Blaeu. Thus, for every visitor, not only the world, but also the sky was at their feet: Amsterdam as the centre of the universe. Since 1815, the building has been used as the official reception palace of the Dutch Royal Family.

National Monument

The National Monument on Dam Square was unveiled on 4 May 1956 as a memorial to all World War II victims. The monument, designed by architect J.J.P. Oud (1890-1963), consists of a 22-metre-high column and a semi-circular memorial wall of white Italian travertine. A female figure with child and the doves symbolize peace and new life. The sculptures were designed by John Rädecker (1885-1956) and his sons Han and Jan Willem, the reliefs by Paul Grégoire (1915-1988).

Beursplein/Damrak 243
H.P. Berlage
1884-1903
L. Zijl, J. Mendes da Costa, R.N. Roland
Holst, A.J. Derkinderen, J.Th. Toorop (art)

Architect J.D. Zocher's 1845
Commodity Exchange was too small
and inconveniently located in the
middle of Dam Square. Therefore, as
early as the late 1870s, a number of
architects submitted new plans, solici-
ted and unsolicited, for various locations. A competition was launched
in 1884, which came to nothing after
199 entries and a second round for
five selected design teams (including Berlage). Thanks to alderman
Willem Treub's diligence, architect
Hendrik Petrus Berlage (1856-1934)
was commissioned to design a new
sketch plan (without facades) in 1896.
In 1898, he received the final commission for a new exchange building.
The plan layout was already largely
fixed and determined by functional

requirements. The design was based
on a geometric system of proportions.
For the facades, Berlage used the
so-called Egyptian triangle: the ratio
5:8. The floor plans were based on a
practical module of 3.80 metres.
What is striking about the exterior is its
high degree of unity. The various functions, such as offices, entrances and
the three large halls for goods, cer-
eals and stock, were subordinated to
the totality of the facade. The long,
straight facade on the Damrak forms
a continuous plane with window sections, enlivened by vertical elements.
In the east facade, the large rectangular halls meet the sloping building line.
Berlage used many means to accen-
tuate this play of lines, including low
structures along the building line and a
double facade. The two short facades
are more like a collection of separate
building parts. On the south side, the
tower is placed asymmetrically with
respect to the main entrance. The
north facade is very fragmentary and,
because the grain exchange is far back

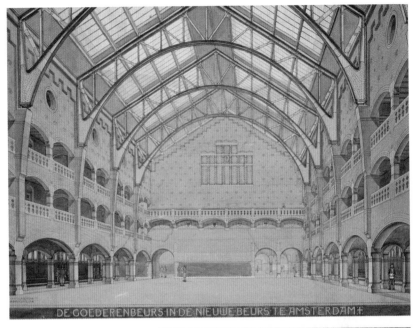

DE GOEDERENBEURS IN DE NIEUWE BEURS TE AMSTERDAM.

and only closed with a low gallery, has a large 'hole' in the facade wall. The large halls are spanned by curved steel trusses which have been left in sight. In the interior, glazed brick has been used extensively. Ornamentation is incorporated into the overall composition of the building and is often an expression of a function, such as natural stone consoles, keystones and lintels, hinges, locks and drains. Numerous well-known artists such as Jan Toorop, Lambertus Zijl and Joseph Mendes da Costa contributed to the decoration.

In Dutch architecture, the Exchange and Berlage have become synonyms for the dawn of modern architecture. Built on the border of two centuries, the building represents a transition from neo-styles and art nouveau to pragmatism, from fantasy and romanticism to rationalism. The work served as a model for both the architects of the Amsterdam School and the moderns. But the traditionalist Alexander Kropholler also took its brick use and Romanesque forms as inspiration.

In 1959, when there was talk of plans to remodel or even demolish the building, the Dutch architectural world protested unanimously. From 1984, trade activities gradually moved to new buildings. Since then, the Beurs van Berlage has had a cultural destination and has been used for exhibitions, conferences and events. The offices have been leased to companies in the cultural sector and the main entrance has been converted into grand café Bistro Berlage.

11 Magna Plaza

☕ 🍴 Ⓗ

Nieuwezijds Voorburgwal 182
C.H. Peters/H.J.L.M. Ruijssenaars
1893-1899/1988-1992
E.A.F. Bourgonjon (art)

Amsterdam's former main post office dating from 1899 is the most important work of government architect Cornelis Peters (1847-1932). Peters, who would build over 40 post offices in the Netherlands, designed this colossal, richly detailed brick building in a mixed style of neo-Gothic and neo-Renaissance. Together with Raadhuisstraat 🔟, the huge building was part of a massive scale-up of Amsterdam's city centre at the turn of the last century. After a conversion by Hans Ruijssenaars (1944) in 1992 into Magna Plaza shopping centre, the entire building was made publicly accessible. With the central element being the monumental hall, surrounded by galleries with sandstone arcades with an impressive void over three floors. In the design, the existing main entrance and monumental staircases were retained and supplemented by two systems of escalators. On both sides of the central hall, separated by the monumental gallery bridges, two new voids of two storeys high were created, enlarging the two existing light courts and covering a third inner courtyard with glass.

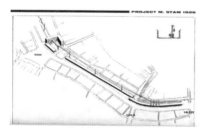

The Rokin Competition

In 1924, the municipality issued a study competition for the Rokin, then a canal between the Dam and Munt squares. Almost all of the entrants, including De Stijl architect Cornelis van Eesteren, wanted the Rokin to be filled in. Revolutionary was Mart Stam's 1926 idea for a series of office buildings on pilotis, which would leave the ground floor free for pedestrians and parking. A propeller-driven cable car would be suspended above the offices. In 1938, part of the Rokin was indeed filled in; instead of buildings – futuristic or otherwise – a car park was realized at the site.

12   W Hotel

Nieuwezijds Voorburgwal 226 ⛊
J. Crouwel jr./Office Winhov
1924-1927/2011-2015

The Government Office for Transactions and Telephony by architect Joseph Crouwel (1885-1962) was built close to the former main post office **11**. An entire building block was demolished for its construction. Around a high central public hall were four floors of offices. The ground floor contained mainly counters. Due to budget cuts, a large glass roof over the hall was not installed. By adding a connection in the middle between the two stairwells, two smaller light courts were created. The design of the building resulted in functional, strongly horizontally oriented facades, with continuous brick parapets, concrete bands and a plinth of natural stone. The building has a concrete skeleton. In 2015, it was converted into a hotel by Office Winhov, the architectural office of Jan Peter Wingender (1965) and Joost Hovenier (1963-2016), with 159 'contemporary lifestyle' rooms, ten suites and one 'extreme wow' suite. A glass roof structure houses the reception, lobby and restaurant and the facades of the inner courts have been given an aluminium bronze construction. One of the vaults on the roof floor has been transformed into a swimming pool.

Houten Huys   ⛊

Tucked away in the bustling shopping area near Kalverstraat is the Begijnhof. It is a beautiful ensemble of late medieval houses, only accessible during the day from the Gedempte Begijnensloot and through a gate on the Spui. Many facades have been renewed over time, but the Houten Huys (Wooden House) at No 34 not only has a wooden frame construction, but also a wooden facade. Recent research has revealed that it dates from around 1530, making it just short of being the oldest house in Amsterdam.

13 P.C. Hoofthuis

Spuistraat 134/Raadhuisstraat
Th.J.J. Bosch
1976-1984

To make this colossal, more than 100-metre-long university building fit in with the scale of the canal wall, architect Theo Bosch (1940-1994) opted for a strongly vertical articulation of the building, with uneven facade sections. The size of the spared corner building called the White House was taken as a starting point. The indentations in the building are not identical, in keeping with the varied facade pattern of the surrounding area. Inside, too, the architect opted for a 'democratic' layout, with corridors designed as indoor streets and break rooms as squares. Through glass walls, passers-by can peek into the lecture halls here. The bright and transparent building, which replaced a gloomy nineteenth-century bank building, is widely regarded as one of the highlights of Dutch structuralism, an architectural movement based on a rigid configuration of the – often concrete – load-bearing structure with a freer interpretation of the remaining building parts. For security reasons, the building's entrances were soon closed off with fences.

Homomonument

As a lasting memorial to gay emancipation, the Homomonument, the first of its kind in the world, was unveiled between the Westerkerk church **17** and the Keizersgracht canal on 5 September 1987. The monument consists of three pink granite triangles, which together form one big triangle. The pink triangle, the symbol of the gay movement since the 1960s, was originally used in Nazi Germany as an identifier for gay prisoners. The monument was designed by Karin Daan (1944).

Raadhuisstraat 21-55
A.L. van Gendt en Zonen
1896-1898
J.H. Schröder (art)

At the end of the nineteenth century, the city expanded westwards. This created a need for a through route between the new neighbourhoods and the city centre. Raadhuisstraat is a thoroughfare between the Herengracht and Keizersgracht canals. In a slight bend, architect Dolf van Gendt (1835-1901) created a shopping arcade with dwellings above it. The client was insurance company

De Utrecht. The eighteen shops line an arcade; in the middle is a different, projecting section with a larger arch. Art Nouveau influences are evident in the many details. The gallery is richly decorated with ornaments and sculptures of animal figures (crocodiles, lions, an eagle) and monsters. These were meant to inspire passers-by to take out a life insurance policy with the commissioner; the letter U of De Utrecht can also be seen throughout.

't Binnenhuis

At Raadhuisstraat 48-50, retail store 't Binnenhuis was built in 1907 to the design of architects J.F. Staal and A.J. Kropholler. Here, contemporary crafts were displayed and sold, by designers such as H.P. Berlage and Jac. van den Bosch. The aim of 'NV tot het ontwerpen, vervaardigen en verkoopen van huisraad Het Binnenhuis' ('LLC to design, manufacture and sell home furnishings Het Binnenhuis') was to make well-designed household goods available to larger groups of people. In 1929, 't Binnenhuis was closed down and Metz **19** took over the leading role in the field of modern furniture.

Ring of Canals

Amsterdam's world-famous ring of canals was built around 1600 as a massive urban extension around the old city centre. During this period, the port city of Amsterdam grew into the capital of world trade and its population multiplied from 30,000 in 1580 to 205,000 in 1680. The ring of canals consists of a system of four main canals, the Herengracht, the Keizersgracht, the Prinsengracht and the Singel, built in large concentric belts around the old city centre. This large-scale and planned form of urban expansion was an idea of city architect Hendrick Jacobszoon Staets (1558-1630). The construction of this project, which was unprecedented in the world at the time, took place in four successive phases, with the first two creating a first shell around the medieval city centre. With the Third and Fourth Extensions, realized between 1613 and 1672, the ring of canals that has defined the city's characteristic appearance was created.

The city council of the time, consisting mainly of wealthy merchants, added aesthetic principles to the canal project alongside commercial and practical ones. For instance, all bridges were made of stone, an admittedly expensive but low-maintenance solution that was also attractive for the residents. Trees were planted along all canals, which not only

Map of Amsterdam showing the Third Extension and the design for the Fourth Extension, printed and published in 1662 by Frederik de Wit.

Construction of the Golden Bend on the Herengracht, in a 1672 painting by Gerrit Adriaenszoon Berkheyde.

provided shade but also strengthened the quay walls. The canals were furthermore laid out as much as possible in straight stretches with a limited number of kinks, so that efficient rectangular building plots could be sold to interested merchants. These plots were relatively narrow because of the tax levied on the width of the frontage, and extended deep to halfway down the next canal. Gardens were laid out in these courtyards, but there was also room for additional construction in the form of so-called 'rear annexes' **16**.

From the outset, the ring of canals was where wealthy Amsterdammers lived and worked, as they used the canals to transport their trade goods. Merchant houses often combined living and working, with a storage space in the basement, an elevated ground floor, one or more living floors and an attic with further storage space. The construction of the first canal houses generally did not involve a designer or master builder. Local carpenters and bricklayers provided an often uniform design of the merchant houses with a narrow, relatively tall brick facade and a crow-stepped gable as the standard crowning feature. Only in later centuries did the Canal District acquire its current variety of facades through conversions and functional adaptations.

The very rich could afford to buy two plots and build a double-wide canal house there. These were mainly found in the so-called Golden Bend on the Herengracht between Leidsestraat and Vijzelstraat. There are 230 listed buildings in the ring of canals, a number of which can be visited, including the double-wide Bartolotti House (H. de Keyser, 1620) **15**, the Anne Frank House (D. van Delft, 1635) **16** and the museums Van Loon, Willet-Holthuysen House, the Museum of the Canals, Foam Photography Museum and Huis Marseille. The ring of canals was placed on the Unesco World Heritage List in 2010.

15   Bartolotti House

🏛 🍺

Herengracht 170-172
H. de Keyser
1620

Bartolotti House was built around 1620 by order of wealthy banker/merchant Willem Bartolotti van den Heuvel (ca. 1560-1634), probably after a design by Amsterdam city architect and sculptor Hendrick de Keyser (1565-1621). The double-width house, richly ornamented with pilasters, medallions, vases, balusters and other sculptures, was one of the largest houses in the city at the time. It was built in a small bend along the Herengracht canal, with the living quarters on the left and the reception rooms in the right-hand section. After it was split in 1755, whaler Jan van Tarelink built a vast rear annexe attached to the right part of the house with a large hall in rococo style. Its stucco is among the finest examples of rococo in the Netherlands.

The right part, restored by the Hendrick de Keyser Association between 1968 and 1971, can now be visited as a museum house. The garden behind is also open to visitors. The text on the reconstructed gable 'Renovata Ao MCMLXXI' refers to the 1971 restoration.

Hendrick de Keyser Association

The left part of Bartolotti House, at number 172, houses the offices of the Hendrick de Keyser Association. The Association is dedicated to preserving historically valuable houses and interiors throughout the Netherlands. Many of their properties can be visited as museum houses or rented for events or as holiday homes. A special feature of their properties is that you are allowed to touch and open everything.

Prinsengracht 263
D. van Delft
1635/1739
Benthem Crouwel (exp. 1993-1999);
Bierman Henket (ren. 2015-2019)

The building at Prinsengracht 263 is best known for its occupants, Anne Frank and her Jewish family, who used it as a hiding place during the Second World War. In the Secret Annex, hidden behind a revolving bookcase, Anne Frank (1929-1945) wrote her world-famous diary. The building, together with the neighbouring house at No 265, was built in 1635 by Dirk van Delft (c. 1591-1658). Because the plots along Amsterdam's canals were expensive and in demand, so-called 'rear annexes' were built on the cheaper courtyards. The one where the Frank family lived between 1942 and 1944 dates from 1739. After the Second World War, there were plans to demolish the building. As more and more people came to know about the diaries, the then owner decided to donate the building. Several neighbouring properties were acquired over the years, after which the Anne Frank House was officially opened as a museum in 1960. In the building at Prinsengracht 263, both the house at the front and the house at the back have been restored to their original state. The interior has been completely reconstructed as it was when the Frank family lived there. The adjacent new building houses the museum entrance and its public functions.

Anne Frank

A bronze statue of Anne Frank, by artist Mari Andriessen (1897-1979), has stood on the nearby Westermarkt on the south side of the Westerkerk church since 1977. Andriessen also hid people in his home during the Second World War, and his studio was used to store weapons for the resistance. Another statue of Anne Frank, created by artist Jet Schepp (1940), stands opposite the house at Merwedeplein 37/2 in Amsterdam-South, where the Frank family lived until they went into hiding in 1942.

17 Westertoren

Prinsengracht 279
H. de Keyser
1620-1638

With its 85 metres, the Westertoren ('western tower') is the tallest church tower in Amsterdam. The Oude Wester (Old Wester), as it is popularly known, has been the subject of songs and writings since its completion in 1638. The tower forms one unit with the Westerkerk, which was built between 1620 and 1631 in Renaissance style by Amsterdam city architect Hendrick de Keyser (1565-1621). Because the tower was also to be used as a lookout post for the fire watch, it is actually too high for the accompanying church. The body of the tower is made of brick. To limit the tower's weight, the floor above it is made of sandstone and the two upper parts are made of wood, clad with lead. Still, the tower has subsided; it is 88 centimetres out of plumb. After Hendrick de Keyser's death in 1621, the tower's design was modified and the top took on a more classicist character. The tower is crowned with the characteristic imperial crown of Amsterdam's city arms.

Aan de voet van die Oude Wester

Famous Amsterdam popular singers Willy Alberti and Johnny Jordaan sang about the Westertoren in the song *Aan de voet van die Oude Wester*. The song was written in 1951 by Tom Erich and Jaap Sjouwerman.

At the foot of that beautiful Wester
I have often stood there thinking
I have often stood there dreaming
Of that beautiful, that fine Jordaan

18   Headquarters EHLB

Keizersgracht 174-176/Leliegracht
G.A. van Arkel
1904-1905
C. Wegener Sleeswijk (exp. 1966-1968);
H.H. Baanders (ass.)

The prolific Amsterdam architect Gerrit van Arkel (1858-1918) took over the commission for a new office building for the Eerste Hollandsche Levensverzekerings Bank (EHLB) from architect Hermanus Baanders in 1903. At the corner of the Keizersgracht and Leliegracht canals, three buildings were demolished and replaced by a six-storey bank building. The building has a concrete frame. There are Art Nouveau details in the facade, such as the wrought-iron structure with the letters EHLB on the roof. Its size and appearance were not to the liking of contemporaries and as late as 1963, the building was referred to as 'an architectural abomination with obtrusive colours'. The two mosaics show a guardian angel with two people, symbolizing the protective role of a life insurance company. In the late 1960s, the building was extended on both sides by Cornelis Wegener Sleeswijk creating a gradual transition from the high blind side walls to the lower canal houses. The building is depicted on at least four tile tableaux: in Amsterdam at Rozengracht 58 and Ceintuurbaan 263, in The Hague at Stationsweg 72 and in Rotterdam at Lombardkade 53.

Geef mij maar Amsterdam

'Geef mij maar Amsterdam, dat is mooier dan Parijs' ('I prefer Amsterdam, it's nicer than Paris'), Johnny Jordaan sang in 1956. The typical Amsterdam chanson-like *levenslied* is also known as Jordaan repertoire. In the middle of the Jordaan neighbourhood, where Elandsgracht and Prinsengracht meet, stands a sculpture group featuring Amsterdam musicians: Johnny Jordaan, Tante Leen, Johnny Meyer, Manke Nelis and Bolle Jan & Mien

Froger. The sculptures were created from 1991 by Kees Verkade (1941-2020).

19 Residential House

Singel 428
A. Cahen
1964-1970

This bold interpretation of the historic canal wall was rejected fourteen times by the building aesthetics committee of the time. In the end, the facade of prefabricated concrete elements was nevertheless realized. Without the perseverance of architect and client, the design would have been caught in 'a web of objections, regulations and stipulations'. The facade has a contemporary character but is in harmony with its environs. The property, which is only 6.20 metres wide, contains a commercial space in the souterrain, an entrance hall and storerooms on the ground floor, three standard flats above and a luxury penthouse with a roof terrace over the two floors. As a playful addition to the 76 identical parapet elements and 25 identical columns, a single round column was used at the entrance. In the architectural world, the project is considered a textbook example of successful new construction in a historical context, but it has hardly been emulated.

Metz & Co.

On the corner of Leidsestraat and Keizersgracht is a retail building best known as Metz & Co furniture shop. Built in 1891 by architect Jan van Looy for the New York Life Insurance Company, it was the tallest private building in Amsterdam at the time with a height of 26 metres. In 1933, architect Gerrit Rietveld (1888-1964) designed a glass showroom cupola on the roof. Metz was of great prominence in introducing modern, functional furniture such as tubular steel chairs, arts and crafts

and home furnishings. The showroom closed in 2013.

Vijzelstraat 32
K.P.C. de Bazel
1919-1926
A.D.N. van Gendt (constr.); J. Mendes da
Costa, L. Zijl, H.A. van den Eijnde (art);
Claus & Kaan (ren. 2003-2007)

The robust and closed former head office of the Nederlandsche Handel-Maatschappij was designed by architect Karel de Bazel (1869-1923) as a gesamtkunstwerk, in which he also designed all interior elements, including the furniture. The outer walls of the colossal building, although 75 centimetres thick, are neither intended nor executed as load-bearing walls. The building has a concrete skeleton, designed by Dolf van Gendt. Inside, this gives the building a very different character: the interior is bright and clean. The floor plan around the two glass-covered light courts is based on a grid of 3.60 by 3.20 metres. These dimensions were taken from the desks at which bank staff stood to do their work at the time. For the benefit of the new user, the Amsterdam City Archives, the building's accessibility was improved in 2007 by, among other things, fitting the niches at the entrances with glass and accommodating public functions (information centre, city bookshop, café) in the lower building layers.

Het Lieverdje

The cigarette manufacturer-sponsored statue Het Lieverdje ('The Little Darling') at Spui square, a design by Amsterdam sculptor Carel Kneulman (1915-2008), became the centre of the happenings of the Provo movement around 'anti-smoking magician' Robert Jasper Grootveld in the 1960s. At the time, the Provos took playful action against the establishment, making them pioneers in the field of political and cultural democratization and emancipation. Photographer Peter

Dicampos took this seminal photo in 1967, with artist Phil Bloom posing in front of it with a concealing bunch of red tulips.

Reguliersbreestraat 26-28
H.L. de Jong
1918-1921
C. Bartels, B. Jordens, J.W. Gidding (int.)

In sharp contrast to the austere Cineac cinema **22**, which was built almost at the same time, the Tuschinski Theatre is in an exuberant Art Deco style designed by Hijman Louis de Jong (1882-1942). Initiator Abraham Tuschinski (1886-1942) wanted 'the grandest of the grandest' on this site and realized an extremely luxurious cinema with an imposing facade, richly decorated and clad entirely in glazed tiles, ceramic sculptures, wrought-iron decorations and bronze lamps. The interior, especially the lobby, also features artistic decorations such as carpets, wall and ceiling paintings, lighting effects and furniture, most of which have been well-preserved. The luxuriously appointed large theatre auditorium with two projecting balconies originally accommodated nearly 1,600 visitors. Opinions about the building were mixed even upon completion. According to the *Bouwkundig Weekblad* ('Architecture Weekly'), 'the cityscape was completely spoiled' by the 'shapeless towers' in 'the shape of a 42 cm projectile'. In 2021, the building was declared 'the most beautiful cinema in the world' by leading British cultural magazine *Time Out*.

Amsterdamned

Amsterdam is a prime location for film shoots. What could be better than a spectacular chase through the canals, as in *Puppet On A Chain* from 1970, *Amsterdamned* from 1988 or *Black Lotus* from 2023. The city is particularly popular for crime films: in 2004, Brad Pitt and George Clooney visited Amsterdam for *Oceans 12*. The 1971 Bond film *Diamonds Are Forever* has a scene at the Magere Brug ('Skinny Bridge'). The bench in front of Leliegracht 4 in *The Fault in Our Stars* from 2014 was briefly a place of pilgrimage for this film's fans.

22   Cineac

H

Reguliersbreestraat 31-33
J. Duiker
1933-1934

The most distinctive part of this iconic design by architect Jan Duiker (1890-1935), one of the pioneers of the *Nieuwe Bouwen* modern architecture movement, are the neon light advertisements in the constructivist steel roof structure and on the facade. The grey steel facade panels are interspersed with large glass panes. Above the entrance area with its glass canopy was a glass booth behind which film projectors were visible from the street. Unlike the Tuschinski Theatre across the street **21**, the Cineac was built as a newsreel cinema, where visitors could enter at any time of the day to watch the daily news in a continuous one-hour film screening. The word Cineac is derived from 'cinema' and 'actualité'. The building has since lost its function and has undergone major changes, especially in the interior.

Art-Deco Cinemas

Cinemas are usually buildings with a closed facade without windows. In the heyday of cinema, the 1920s and 1930s, many Art Deco facades were realized. As at the former Ceintuurtheater (Ceintuurbaan 282) from 1921 by architect Willem Noorlander with a concrete facade. And the 1920 Rialto cinema (Ceintuurbaan 338) by Jan van Schaik. Cinema Desmet (Plantage Middenlaan 4a) was originally a theatre. In 1927, architect Jan Boterenbrood gave it an Art Deco facade. It is still in use as a cinema.

☕ 🍴

Kleine-Gartmanplantsoen 15-19
J. Wils
1934-1935

By choosing an efficient steel-framed construction method for the construction of this large cinema, the imposing City Theatre could be both designed and built in a timeframe of less than a year. With a large horseshoe-shaped auditorium with a balcony, architect Jan Wils (1891-1972) created a modern cinema that seated a hundred people more than Tuschinski Theatre 21, which had been realized earlier. Wils may have based his design on an earlier

design by Jan Duiker, the architect of the Cineac 22. An icon of modernity, the building was equipped with the latest innovations in technology, acoustics and climate control right from its completion. It also had a sprinkler system. With its clean yellow brick facade, distinctive lettering, crowned glass tower with winding stairs and vertical lighting, the building has acted as a beacon in the nightlife around Leidseplein for almost a century. The large cinema auditorium has been divided into seven smaller auditoriums during several renovations.

Paradiso & Melkweg

There are two famous music venues around Leidseplein. The Church of the Free Congregation (G.B. Salm, 1879-1880) at Weteringschans 6-8 has housed the 'cosmic relaxation centre' Paradiso since March 1968. Some of the world's biggest music acts performed at this legendary pop temple, such as Pink Floyd, Captain Beefheart, The Rolling Stones, Prince and David Bowie. Melkweg (Lijnbaansgracht 234a) developed more as a hippie venue in an old milk factory from 1970.

24 Hotel Café Restaurant American

Leidseplein 28
W. Kromhout Czn., H.G. Jansen
1898-1902
L. Nienhuis (art), G.J. Rutgers (exp. 1928)

The famous Amsterdam American Hotel, pronounced 'Américain' by everyone in the French way, contained a famous café-restaurant on the ground floor and party rooms on the first floor, in addition to 75 hotel rooms. These different functions of the building were each given their own expression in the facade. A horizontal loggia forms the transition from the arches of the café hall to the vertical character of the hotel facades. A prominent round turret accentuates the corner. There were three entrances: a quiet one for the hotel guests, a prominent one for the café-restaurant and a necessary one for the party rooms. Eastern architecture and Art Nouveau influences can be seen in the decorations, ironwork, tile panels and light fittings. As it happens, architect Willem Kromhout (1864-1940) did not appreciate this 'style of seaweed swirls' at all. In 1928, the building was extended with a new wing designed by Amsterdam School architect Gerrit Jan Rutgers (1877-1962).

Byzantium

For a long time, Rem Koolhaas (1944) had the reputation of being a 'paper architect', making beautiful drawings but not actually building anything. One of his first realized projects is the luxury apartment complex Byzantium on Stadhouderskade, next to the Vondelpark 59. On completion in 1991, there was some disappointment among the trade press and public: rather crudely detailed property developer architecture for the nouveau riche. With the only special feature being the golden projection of the penthouse at the top. But the complex blends in well with the

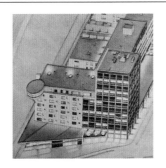

streetscape and forms a natural transition between the metropolitan centre and the park.

History of Amsterdam

Around 1275, the construction of a dam in the Amstel River constituted a major step in the development of the town 'Ammestelledamme'. The dam was equipped with locks, allowing the city to grow into a major port with both an inland harbour (today's Rokin) and a seaport (today's Damrak). With the current Dam as its central trading square, Amsterdam was granted city rights in 1306. The population tripled to 3,000 around 1400. Besides being a city of trade, Amsterdam also became a religious centre with over twenty monasteries and a number of churches, of which the Oude Kerk ('Old Church', 1306) and the Nieuwe Kerk ('New Church', 1408) can still be visited.

With the fall of Antwerp in 1585 a time of unprecedented prosperity and cultural boom began for Amsterdam. Until then, Antwerp had been the most important port and trading city in the region, but with the Spanish conquest of the city and the mass exodus of its population, Amsterdam took over that position. Amsterdam became a centre of art, science and tolerance, attracting intellectuals, merchants and artists from all over the world; by 1600, one in three people in Amsterdam were immigrants. After the great successes of the first expeditions to sail the world's seas, the Vereenigde Oostindische Compagnie (United East India Company, or VOC) was founded in 1602, which would grow into the largest trading and shipping

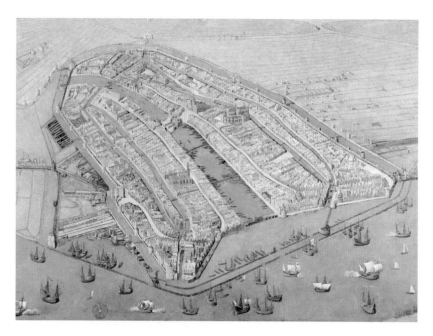

Amsterdam in 1538. This map, made by Cornelis Anthoniszoon, is the oldest city map of Amsterdam. It shows the completed medieval Amsterdam (with city wall and gates).

company in the world. To emphasize Amsterdam's great might, the city council commissioned Jacob van Campen to build the largest city hall in the world – the current Royal Palace on Dam Square ⑨. In a period of less than a hundred years, the construction of the ring of canals enlarged the city by more than five times.

In the centuries that followed, the typical crescent shape of the ring of canals continued to define Amsterdam's map. It wasn't until the mid-nineteenth century that Amsterdam would start building again. At that time, Amsterdam was

Densely populated and impoverished working-class houses around 1930 in the Zwarte Bijlsteeg.

thriving as an industrial city. The construction of the North Sea Canal in 1876 re-established the city's direct connection to the sea. Besides new residential areas outside the ring of canals such as De Pijp and those around the chic Vondelpark 59, the city also gained new cultural prestige with the construction of the Rijksmuseum 25, the Stedelijk Museum 27 and the Concertgebouw 29.

While the population doubled from around 250,000 in 1850 to 510,000 in 1900, the number of houses lagged considerably behind and the available housing became overcrowded. These social ills made Amsterdam a centre of Dutch social democracy at the beginning of the twentieth century. With a new administrative culture, this led to two major urban expansions: Plan Zuid 63 (1915) and the General Expansion Plan (1935). Amsterdam has since continued to play an important role in terms of progressive culture, tolerance and diversity, and as a cradle of social change, such as the policy of tolerance regarding soft drugs and same-sex marriage 13. Amsterdam's population has almost doubled again over the past hundred years to 920,000 in 2023. The number of housing units has quadrupled over this period from 120,000 in 1900 to 480,000 units in 2023.

25 Rijksmuseum

Museumstraat 1
P.J.H. Cuypers
1875-1885
G. Sturm, B.J.W.M. van Hove, W.F. Dixon,
J.F. Vermeylen, A. Hesselink (art);
Cruz & Ortiz (ren. 2001-2013)

The national museum Rijksmuseum is one of the largest museums in the Netherlands. It is best known for its large collection of paintings from the seventeenth century, with works by Rembrandt van Rijn, Johannes Vermeer and Frans Hals. The building dates from 1885 and was designed by one of the most important Dutch architects of the nineteenth century: Pierre Cuypers (1827-1921). His design for the museum was inspired by late Gothic

and early Renaissance styles. In its historicizing form language, the building pays homage to Dutch art and history of the sixteenth and seventeenth centuries. The massive building, one of Cuypers' biggest commissions, has a classic symmetrical layout with two covered courtyards and a central gallery. The building is designed as a monumental gateway to the new South district of the city, with a passage for through traffic in the middle. Above this passage in the middle axis of the building is the gallery of honour with masterpieces of Dutch painting, with a Cuypers-designed view through to the Night Watch, Rembrandt's largest painting. Like the French architect Viollet-le-Duc, from whom he had taken a few classes, Cuypers applied

Self-portrait

Just as master builders did in the Middle Ages to adorn their magnificent cathedrals, architect Pierre Cuypers created a sculpted portrait of himself on the outside of the Rijksmuseum. The bearded architect can be seen with an antique stone lifter in his hand on a corner of the left tower next to the extension on the Museum Square side.

The museum was given a new entrance in the two restored inner courtyards on either side of the passage. Lowering the floor created a large and bright underground plaza here. The Portuguese natural stone of the floor and entrance gates matches the beige limestone used by Cuypers in the facades of the inner courts. Modern chandeliers hang from the cast-iron roof structure to improve acoustics and lighting. At the new entrances in the passage, Cuypers' brick walls have given way to large glass walls, which now give passersby a direct view of the underground plaza. The architects also created a few extensions, including the Asian pavilion.

Gothic construction principles in his design. For instance, the halls and corridors of the museum are spanned with masonry rib vaults. Cuypers not only designed the building, but also the extensive decoration programme with a plethora of ornaments, paintings, mosaic floors, stained-glass windows, ironwork, tile tableaux and sculptures. Between 2003 and 2013, the museum was restored to its former glory by Spanish architects Antonio Cruz (1948) and Antonio Ortiz (1947).

Outdoor Museum

In his design for the Rijksmuseum in 1901, Cuypers also designed the gardens surrounding the museum. In this outdoor museum, he placed (fragments of) historic Dutch buildings threatened with demolition, such as the Groninger Herenpoort from 1621. New in the collection are the famous telephone booth by Brinkman & Van der Vlugt from 1933, and playground equipment by Aldo van Eyck from 1962: a climbing tower and funnel, a climbing dome and four tumbling bars, from Slotermeer **45**.

Museumplein 6
Rietveld Van Dillen Van Tricht
1963-1973
K. Kurokawa (exp. 1989-1999);
J.J.H.M. van Heeswijk (exp. 2015)

With more than two hundred paintings, the museum holds the largest collection of works by the famous Dutch painter Vincent van Gogh (1853-1890). The museum consists of two buildings. As with the adjacent Stedelijk Museum **27**, the museum's entrance was moved to the new development side on Museum Square in 2015. The old building on Paulus Potterstraat, an open spatial composition with a large central void over the full height of the building, was designed by architect Gerrit Rietveld (1888-1964) in 1963. The museum was expanded in 1999 with an elliptical natural stone exhibition building by Japanese architect Kisho Kurokawa (1934-2007). The design of this Kurokawa wing was completed in 2015 with the construction of a new glass entrance building with a sunken foyer housing the public facilities and a museum shop. From this bright underground space, both buildings can be accessed, the Rietveld building with the permanent Van Gogh collection and the Kurokawa wing for temporary exhibitions.

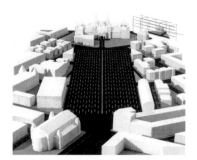

Shortest motorway in the Netherlands

In a 1988 ideas competition asking whether Museum Square should remain an open space and whether the narrow and busy carriageway in the middle of the square should be removed, artist John Körmeling (1951) suggested asphalting Museum Square and making it the shortest and widest motorway in the Netherlands.

Museumplein 10
A.W. Weissman; Benthem Crouwel
1891-1895; 2004-2012

After years of discussion, the Stedelijk Museum in Renaissance Revival style by city architect Adriaan Weismann (1858-1923) was given an extension by Benthem Crouwel in the form of a large underground hall and a striking white above-ground building section. As a result, the existing museum building remained in view. By placing the museum's new entrance on Museum Square, the organizational structure of the old building has been turned 180 degrees, just like the Van Gogh Museum 26. The white floating volume, popularly referred to as 'the Bathtub', created a covered plaza that smoothly flows into the bright reception hall as the museum's vestibule. Despite the stark contrast between the old and new building, all spaces inside flow seamlessly into one another. The famous staircase in the old building and the natural lighting in the galleries have been preserved, as well as the revolutionary colour white that then-director Willem Sandberg introduced in the museum in 1938.

Mural

In 1956, in the former restaurant of the Stedelijk Museum, Cobra artist Karel Appel (1921-2006) painted a ten-metre-wide wall with three cheerful and colourful figures: a crested bird, a human figure and a flower. Since he didn't quite manage to fit them all on this wall, he also painted on the wall next to it. The doorways and the coloured-glass oval window made using the appliqué technique are part of the composition.

P.C. Hooftstraat 94-96
MVRDV
2012-2016

For this double storefront in the capital's glamorous shopping street, MVRDV designed an unusual facade: built with bricks in the traditional way, but made of glass. To comply with municipal regulations, the glass brick facade gradually transitions to a regular brick facade towards the upper floors. The solid architraves and window frames are also in glass. A special aspect of the glass facade is that it has a normal load-bearing function. Other buildings on this shopping street are also getting architectural facelifts. At No 138 is The Looking Glass with three storey-high curved glass panels in the facade (UN Studio, 2017-2019). The Rose House at No 45 (Studio Job, 2020) has a polished bronze facade with cast roses 'growing' down from planters. At No 32, a 3D-printed facade can be seen on the Ceramic House (Studio RAP, 2021-2023). The sculptural brick facade of The Lady (Dok architects, 2023) at No 123 is the architects' homage to city sculptor Hildo Krop.

The Rose House

The Looking Glass

29   Concertgebouw

☕ 🍴

Van Baerlestraat 98
A.L. van Gendt
1883-1886
J. Franse (art); P.B. de Bruijn (exp.
1984-1988)

The Concertgebouw's acoustics are
ranked among the best in the world.
The building was designed by architect Dolf van Gendt (1835-1901) based
on the Neues Gewandhaus in Leipzig,
which had opened in 1884 and was
destroyed during the Second World
War. The acoustics are so exceptional
that subsequent restorations have left
the building's original detailing intact
as much as possible. The building has

four halls: the Main Hall, the Recital
Hall, the Choir Hall and the Mirror Hall.
The building in Renaissance Revival
style has a facade with a classicist row
of columns crowned by a 16-metre-
wide pediment. Central to the relief is
the muse of music, holding a lyre. On
the roof, there is another lyre, gilded
and over three metres high, emblem-
atic of the Concertgebouw. A major
renovation in 1988 saw a new main
entrance built on the left side with a
modern glass foyer, designed by architect Pi de Bruijn (1942).

Beach Boys

On 18 December 1970, a performance by
The Beach Boys at the Concertgebouw
was scheduled around midnight. Due to
dense fog at Schiphol Airport, their plane
from London had to divert to Brussels,
after which the American band was taken
by taxis to Amsterdam. The audience
faithfully waited and at five in the morn-
ing, the concert began. The Beach Boys
found the Netherlands so special that
they ended up living here for six months
in 1972 to record the album *Holland*.
Featuring a typical Dutch houseboat on
the cover.

Overhoeksplein 1
A. Staal
1967-1971
Claus Van Wageningen (ren. 2014-2016)

In 1971, on the north bank of the IJ, this eye-catching office tower was built for Shell employees. Architect Arthur Staal (1907-1993) placed the building with its characteristic shape diagonally on the IJ bank. With its 79 metres, it was one of the tallest civil engineering buildings in Amsterdam at the time. In 2016, architects Felix Claus (1956) and Dick van Wageningen (1971) transformed the 15-storey office tower into the multifunctional A'dam Tower, which houses music industry businesses, a hotel and several bars and restaurants, including one that rotates. The new tower retains the features of the original design: a robust, dark tower some distance from the centre, supported by four light sculptural pilotis and crowned with a striking white, twisted crown. The most notable novelty is the viewing platform; Europe's highest swing here lets you float almost a hundred metres above the city.

Tolhuistuin

Next to the office tower for Shell, architect Arthur Staal built a company restaurant in the Tolhuistuin a few years later (1976). In his design, Staal sought to tie in with the leading architectural movement of the 1970s: structuralism. The tented roofs provide an attractive view from the office tower and create a distinctive interior. The Tolhuistuin has been a cultural destination since 2014, with music venue Paradiso 23 being its most famous user.

IJpromenade 1
Delugan Meissl
2005-2012

The striking white building for the film museum on the north bank of the IJ is designed like a sculpture. The white, crystalline shape reflects light in ever-changing ways, giving the building a different appearance at any time of day. With this 'play of light and movement', the museum building refers directly to cinematography, according to Viennese architect couple Roman Delugan (1963) and Elke Meissl (1959). The building, clad in white aluminium panels, does not have a single right angle neither inside nor outside. A scenic route with long, low-rise stairs leads visitors under a sculpturally overhanging building section into the large central foyer. This foyer provides access to four cinemas, a large exhibition space, a museum shop and the offices. The 30-metre-long overhang houses the large auditorium. The ascending, tribune-like central foyer with waterside café-restaurant and terrace offers panoramic views of the old city.

Bridge

A bridge across the IJ has been talked about in Amsterdam since 1839. It remains non-existent, but plans are still being made for one today. Several designs by contractor/architect Jan Galman (1807-1891) are known, including this one from 1857 with a clearance of 21 metres. Warehouses were situated under the ramps, with a double row of residential houses above them along the road.

Meeuwenlaan/Noordwal/IJplein
R.L. Koolhaas, J.H.B. Voorberg (OMA)
1980-1982

IJplein is one of the first realized projects of the Office for Metropolitan Architecture (OMA). At a prime location on the IJ, the office of Rem Koolhaas (1944) created a small, colourful residential area with social housing. Built on the former yard of the ship-repair company Amsterdamsche Droogdok Maatschappij (ADM), the project tried to fit in with the low-rise building tradition of the nearby garden cities. The project consists of two neighbourhoods: an urban section with elongated residential buildings and 'urban villas' in the west and a villagelike section with low-rise strips of houses and collective gardens in the east. In the urban development plan, OMA laid down not only the location and overall shape of the buildings, but also the colour of the facades. Several architectural firms have been involved in the elaboration of the buildings. The easternmost building block, a smaller section and a parallel, elongated raised residential building with characteristic staircases, as well as a community centre and supermarket in separate triangular volumes on the ground floor, were designed by OMA itself.

Vogeldorp

Vogeldorp ('Bird village') is the oldest garden village in Amsterdam North. It was built in 1918 by the Municipal Housing Service, which was set up specifically to provide good and affordable housing. The symmetrically designed Vogeldorp consists of over three hundred houses around the central Vogelplein square. The Amsterdam School architect Berend Boeyinga's (1886-1969) design was based on the garden city concept of the Brit Ebenezer Howard.

33 Buikslotermeer

Het Hoogt, Het Laagt, Benedenlangs,
Bovenover, Het Breed
F.J. van Gool
1962-1968

From a study competition with Aldo van Eyck (who withdrew) and Van den Broek & Bakema, the plan by architect Frans van Gool (1922-2015) was chosen. The ten residential buildings have a similar height and layout. On the ground floor are storage rooms and flats. Two maisonettes are accessible from the elevated residential street on the third floor. These residential streets are connected by aluminium overhead bridges, similar to the jetways at Schiphol Airport. Because of the urban character of the neighbourhood, a deliberate choice was made for uniformity in the building blocks and anonymity in the facades. The facades consist of prefabricated concrete elements, filled in with aluminium fronts and wooden frames at the balconies and residential streets. The balconies are partly built-in and have a convex concrete balustrade. A similar convex balustrade is also used at the galleries. There are squares for parking and large green areas between the hook-shaped building blocks.

Bachelorette Flat

Former teen idol and rock 'n' roll singer, fun-loving Ria Valk sang the saucy song *Vrijgezellenflat* ('Bachelorette Flat') into the charts in 1969:

In my little bachelorette flat
I've got quite a plan
Every night a fine man...
go or tangerine

Ria Valk did not live in Amsterdam North, but in a bungalow in Vinkeveen. She was not a bachelor, either, as she got married in 1962. And the flats in the Plan Van Gool were not intended for bachelors, but for families. Still, it is a wonderful record cover, a perfect symbiosis of image and music.

Johan van Hasseltkade 201-259
Space & Matter i.c.w. various architects
2008-2020

Ten years after this collective civic initiative was established, the first houseboats of this sustainable floating housing estate were moored in place in 2018. The neighbourhood consists of 46 water houses spread over 30 water lots, interconnected by five T-shaped, wide wooden jetties that function as residential streets. These are publicly accessible. The master plan was designed by the Space & Matter studio of architects Sascha Glasl (1977), Tjeerd Haccou (1978) and Marthijn Pool (1980). They also developed design rules for the individual dwellings, which the residents commissioned various architects to develop. The residences in this sustainable self-sufficient community are well insulated and equipped with solar panels. A smart grid allows residents to exchange their generated solar power. Heat exchangers derive heating and cooling from the surrounding water.

De Ceuvel

On an abandoned and polluted piece of land at nearby Korte Papaverweg 4, creative hub De Ceuvel was set up in 2014 according to an urban plan by Space & Matter in collaboration with several design studios. As there was no money for decontamination of the polluted soil, the site was planted with soil-cleaning plant species and was then 'built on' with pontoons and old houseboats which, when the lease period is over, can simply be returned to the water.

35 Kraanspoor

Kraanspoor 12-58
OTH Architects
1997-2007

On a 270-metre-long former harbour craneway, architect Trude Hooykaas (1942) designed a floating 3-storey transparent building. The concrete craneway, designed in 1952 by architect J.D. Postma, was originally used as a platform for two cranes. The added volume has a subdued design that emphasizes its industrial past. The glass superstructure with a slender steel structure floats sixteen metres above the water and three metres above its base. The redevelopment of the Kraanspoor, which was once part of one of the largest shipyards in the world, the Nederlandsche Dok en Scheepsbouw Maatschappij (NDSM), acted as a catalyst for the development of the entire former NDSM yard. The Scheepsbouwloods (shipbuilding hall), the Hellingbaan (slipway), the Smederij (forge), the Timmerwerkplaats (carpentry workshop) and the Lasloods (welding hall) have also been preserved and given a new cultural purpose. In the near future, the area will transform into an urban area with over 4,000 homes and commercial spaces.

Dans le Port d'Amsterdam

In a popular and famous 1964 hit song, the Belgian singer Jacques Brel sings to a rousing crescendo about the romantic experiences, boozing and erotic adventures of sailors in the red-light district of the port city of Amsterdam. The song was actually about Antwerp but the two syllables in *Dans le Port d'Anvers* did not fit the metre of the melody. In 1973, David Bowie recorded an English-language version of the song.

IJdok
Van Gameren Mastenbroek
1998-2013

On an artificial island in the IJ is the IJDock. The master plan is by urban planners Dick van Gameren (1962) and Bjarne Mastenbroek (1964). They also designed the underground car park, the marina and the 'public street'. The overall building mass with a height of 44 metres has five incisions, based on lines of sight and vistas, for example in the direction of film museum Eye **31**.

This has created all kinds of irregular volumes reminiscent of the Flatiron Building in New York, which house various functions. Claus & Kaan are responsible for the Palace of Justice on the easternmost tip of the island. The 300-room hotel was designed by architect duo Jan Bakers and Ben Loerakker. The apartments and offices, including those for the National Water Police, are by Zeinstra van Gelderen.

Swing Bridge Restaurant

A new residential area was built on a former shunting yard west of Central Station between 2000 and 2009. The only reminder of the railway past is a steel railway swing bridge from 1922, which stands on a rotating pillar in its opened state. By removing the counterweight and installing an additional gantry structure, a restaurant designed by Pi de Bruijn (1942) could be built on the bridge deck in 2008.

Marnixstraat 250
Zanstra, Gmelig Meyling, De Clercq Zubli
1966-1972

At the edge of the ring of canals, a car park of six floors plus the roof for a total of 650 cars was built in the late 1960s. The ground floor is extra high so that buses can drive here. The robust concrete skeleton has a bay dimension of 10.80 metres. The entry and exit ramps are located in a double cylindrical ramp at the rear. The operation was initially a fiasco; as it was still possible to park for free in the surrounding area, the garage had an occupancy rate of two per cent. Interest in Brutalism brought a renewed appreciation for the photogenic building. Under the ramps on the Singelgracht side came café-restaurant Waterkant in 2014. Prior to that, there was a homeless shelter here.

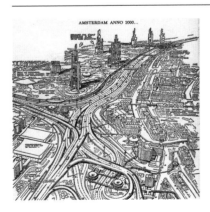

Give the City a Chance

In 1967, American urban planner David A. Jokinen was invited by the car lobby club Stichting Weg to create a vision for the future of Amsterdam. The city centre was to become more accessible to motorists. In the publication *Geef de stad een kans* ('Give the city a chance'), he advocated for the demolition of De Pijp and the Kinkerbuurt neighbourhood and the filling in of the Singel canal in favour of a six-lane motorway with car parks on the outskirts of the city. A new central hub station with a business centre was to be built south of the city centre.

38 Silodam

Silodam 200-459
MVRDV
1995-2002

Next to two former grain silo buildings converted into live/work buildings, architectural firm MVRDV realized an apartment building similar in size and architectural appearance in 2002. The nine-storey building looks like a pile of stacked containers. The complex contains 160 different dwellings of all shapes and sizes: patio houses, lofts, maisonettes, studios and penthouses. Because of the large number of housing types, each with a different size, depth and height, the architects opted for a clustering in units of four to eight similar dwellings. These units were not only given their own expression in the interior with a colourful shared corridor, hallway, gallery or staircase. In the facade too, each unit is recognizable by its own window arrangement and different types of cladding. The entire building is detached from the quay wall. There is a public terrace accessible via a wide staircase running under the building.

Reuse

In 1898, an imposing silo building was constructed in the port of Amsterdam for the bulk storage of grain. The 105-metre-long brick building was designed by architects J.F. Klinkhamer and A.L. van Gendt in an eclectic, neo-Gothic style. In 1952, the complex was expanded with a modern, 37-metre-high concrete silo building by J.D. Postma. To preserve these two image-defining silo buildings for the city, architect André van Stigt carefully converted them into live/work buildings in the late 1990s.

Pontsteiger 2-343
Arons & Gelauff
2006-2019

'An iconic residential building on the IJ' was the brief given to the competition participants for this 90-metre-high building on the waterfront. The new firm of Floor Arons (1968) and Arnoud Gelauff (1963) designed an inviting sculptural residential building that was not located on, but rather in the IJ, thus making even more contact with the water. Since in regular high-rise buildings dwellings in the middle section are the least popular, the architects designed a building with many dwellings at the top and bottom, and very few dwellings in the tower legs in between. This resulted in the distinctive chair shape of the Pontsteiger ('ferry pier'). To bring urban life into the building, the residential building has been elevated using pilotis seven metres in height, with a number of distinctive pavilions under the main form. For the bricks in the facades, a special glaze was developed in collaboration with Royal Tichelaar, which allows the building to change colour depending on the weather: light when the clouds are grey and golden when the sun sets.

REM Island

In the early 1960s, so-called 'pirate stations' provided commercial radio and television broadcasts from ships and oil platforms outside territorial waters. Radio London and Radio Caroline were aimed at Britain, Radio Veronica at the Netherlands. The REM (Reclame Exploitatie Maatschappij, or Advertising Exploitation Company) broadcast popular television series between August and December 1964. Since 2011, the REM Island with a restaurant and viewing platform has been located at Haparandadam 45-2 in the Houthavens ('wood docks').

40   The Ship

Spaarndammerplantsoen,
Oostzaanstraat 45
M. de Klerk
1917-1920
H.L. Krop (art)

Commissioned by cooperative housing association Eigen Haard ('our own
hearth'), architect Michel de Klerk
(1884-1923) designed three building
blocks in the Spaarndammer neighbourhood. The last one, on a triangular
plot on the Spaarndammerplantsoen,
would become known as the epitome
of Amsterdam School architecture. The
houses were equipped with every con-
venience and executed in a design
that was exceptionally lavish for social
housing. De Klerk's expressionist style,
only quietly present in the first two
blocks, reached its peak in this imaginative, richly detailed 'workers' palace'.
The symmetrical design of the complex and its plastic composition with
waves and flowing lines soon earned
the block the name 'Het Schip' ('The
Ship'). The block has 102 houses, most
of which have three rooms.
Characteristic features of the building include the imaginative design
with red brick in impressive masonry
bonds, the curved shapes, the architectural, sometimes vertical use of

roof tiles, the expressive window sections, the unusual bay windows, the
sculptural entrance areas, the lettering and the ornaments by sculptor Hildo Krop (1884-1970) that have
been integrated into the architecture.
The facades of the block have different
designs. The horizontally accentuated

On Oostzaanstraat, De Klerk ingeniously integrated an existing school building, which was not to be demolished, into his design with the addition of a third storey. On the north side, in Hembrugstraat, there is a small triangular square dominated by a sword-shaped, tapered tower that only has a decorative function, as is the case with more elements in the complex. A narrow gate in Oostzaanstraat gives access to the courtyard, where a path between the gardens ends at a small meeting building for residents. After De Klerk's untimely death in 1923, a resident wrote in newspaper *Het Volk*: 'He has passed away, the man of our homes. How shall we working-class women remember this stalwart worker, for what he did for our men and children? Is it not as if every stone calls to you: Come all ye workers and rest in your house, which is there for you. Isn't Spaarndammerplein a fairy tale that you dreamed of as a child, because it was something that didn't exist for us children?'

longitudinal facade on the railway side has been kept relatively plain. On the lower south side, a cylindrical facade ending marked the entrance to the post office that was also included in the block, the interior of which was also lavishly designed by De Klerk.

Museum Het Schip

The former school building houses Museum Het Schip, which provides information on the Amsterdam School and the rise of the housing associations. There is a museum flat, a large collection of Amsterdam School street furniture and the fully equipped post office can also be visited. The museum organizes, also elsewhere in the city, guided tours, bicycle tours, walks and workshops.

41   Westergasfabriek 🍽 🍴 🛏 Ⓗ

Haarlemmerweg 2-14
I. Gosschalk
1883-1885

The Westergasfabriek was built in 1883 to extract gas from coal to use for city lighting. The factory, located along the Haarlemmertrekvaart canal for the supply of coal, was immediately expanded into a vast industrial complex with several buildings, gas holders, coal warehouses, machine workshops, transformer houses, purification plants, offices and living quarters, all designed by Amsterdam architect Isaac Gosschalk (1838-1907). The factory complex with red-brick buildings was rationally designed in a Dutch Renaissance Revival style.

From 2003, work began on repurposing the complex and restoring the seventeen preserved monumental buildings under the supervision of architectural firm Braaksma & Roos. These include a cinema in the Ketelhuis (boiler house), a hotel in the Werkplaatsengebouw (workshop building), various catering establishments and exhibition spaces on the site. The impressive column-free round space with the cast-iron ceiling of the Gashouder (gas holder) from 1902 is now used for events and theatre performances. The American landscape architect Kathryn Gustafson designed the surrounding park.

Keith Haring

On the occasion of his solo exhibition at the Stedelijk Museum in 1986, the American artist Keith Haring (1958-1990) realized one of his largest murals on the grounds of the Centrale Markthallen (Central Market Halls) in Amsterdam-West. On the western wall of the then museum depot, Haring made this monumental mural measuring 12 by 15 metres in a single day, standing on a cherry picker. It can be seen from the public road from the car park on Willem de Zwijgerlaan near Karel Doormanstraat.

42   GWL Terrain   ☕ 🍴 🛏

Haarlemmerweg/Van Hallstraat and environs
KCAP, West 8 i.c.w. various architects
1993-1997

On the former municipal water works site, a compact, green and car-free neighbourhood of 600 houses was built in 1997. It was one of the first eco-friendly housing estates in the Netherlands, where preservation of the monumental existing buildings was also central. The master plan by Kees Christiaanse (KCAP) (1953) was filled in at ground level by landscape architect Adriaan Geuze (West 8) (1960). Two tall, meandering residential blocks are situated along the perimeter of the six-hectare neighbourhood

as a wind and noise buffer. The inner area consists of small, separate residential blocks that match the scale of the existing buildings. The residential blocks were designed by different architects, with a common brief to create ground-level houses with their own front doors. For instance, Kees Christiaanse designed an attached 'residential street' on the fifth storey for the peripheral building on Haarlemmerstraat. The former pump building from 1899 houses a café-restaurant and the small octagonal wind kettle house is a mini hotel. The 37-metre-high water tower from 1966 is still in use.

Amsterdome   🅗

The domed roof of the Amsterdome in the Western Docklands is a striking landmark. The geodetic structure, consisting of 1,100 diamond-shaped aluminium plates suspended in an aluminium tubular structure, originally housed the Aviodome aviation museum at Schiphol Airport. It was built in 1971 according to the principles of American visionary Richard Buckminster Fuller (1895-1983). Since 2021, the dome building, fitted with a new interior, has been in use as an event location at Seineweg 2.

Hoofdweg 405-493
H.Th. Wijdeveld
1923-1925

The two 240-metre-long building blocks on Hoofdweg were designed to accompany this traffic route. They are meant to be experienced by the passing motorist: 'The strongly horizontal in my blocks sought to connect with the character of traffic, as "walking" along the streets and canals transitioned into the "speed" of the car.' The endless array of windows and the closed top edge of decorative brickwork in particular emphasize the length of the street. The individual dwelling is completely subordinate to the overall concept. Yet the subtle details, such as the zinc-clad lifting beams, the brick piers in the top edge and the slightly protruding bands of windows, mean it is not a monotonous building block. The endings are also specially designed; on the north side, a raised block forms a kind of city gate. Architect Hendrik Wijdeveld (1885-1987) only designed the facades; the floor plans are by architects Gulden and Geldmaker.

People's Theatre

Besides being a practising architect with a small body of work, Wijdeveld was above all a designer of large-scale visionary fantasies. An alternative Expansion Plan for Amsterdam (1920), a National Park between Amsterdam and Zandvoort (1927) and an international geological research centre 15 kilometres into the earth (1944) testify to his boundless imagination and optimism. Relatively modest was his 1918 plan for a large People's Theatre in the Vondelpark 59. The theatre as the womb of a new community.

44 Mercatorplein

Mercatorplein
H.P. Berlage
1925-1927
W. Patijn, J. van Kampen (reconstruction tower 1991-1994)

The distinctive Mercatorplein square is the heart of Plan West. Berlage, as the nestor of modern architecture, was invited to be part of this project and designed a so-called 'turbine square'. The bayonet shape of the square interrupts the main Hoofdweg thoroughfare, with a gateway with a tower marking the continuation of the road. The blocks consist of 3-storey housing on a substructure of shops with an arcade. The short facades adjacent to the towers are made of red brick; the two long facades are made of yellow brick and fitted with strips of glass bricks. The dwellings have wide balconies with a projecting, pointed extension. In the early 1990s, the square was redesigned and the second tower, demolished in 1961 because of its poor condition, was reconstructed. In 2010, a pavilion by SeARCH was built on the square; two kiosks that Berlage designed were demolished.

Plan West

Plan West was a private initiative to build 6,000 houses. Based on standard floor plans and a uniform concrete load-bearing structure, 13 architects predominantly designed facades. Since brick was prescribed, many gems of Amsterdam School architecture can be found here. A 'Committee of Three' (two architects and the head of Public Works) supervised the architecture and urban planning, ensuring the desired unity of this city district.

Projects:

1	H.P. Berlage	7	F.B. Jantzen Gzn.
2	C.J. Blaauw	8	J. Roodenburgh
3	M. Staal-Kropholler	9	J.M. van der Meij
4	H.Th. Wijdeveld	10	C.F.G. Peters
5	J.M. van der Meij	11	G.J. Rutgers
6	J.F. Staal	12	P.L. Kramer

Urban Development

With the implementation of the Housing Act in 1901, the government assumed a more active role in public housing. In Amsterdam, the first socialist councillor Floor Wibaut (1859-1936) in particular pushed for better housing conditions. Housing associations were also set up to provide better housing, such as the housing association Eigen Haard ('our own hearth'), which realized the housing development on Spaarndammerplantsoen **40** in 1920.

As it became clear at the end of the nineteenth century that Amsterdam could not continue to expand concentrically without limit, architect Hendrik Petrus Berlage (1856-1934) was asked in 1900 to draw up a plan for a large-scale urban expansion on the south side of the city. Plan Zuid **63** was built between 1917 and 1930 in the style of the Amsterdam School in an imposing succession of closed building blocks, main connecting roads, squares and monumental accents. Berlage also designed the layout of streets, green strips and planting. To research Amsterdam's expected growth until the year 2000, the Urban Development Department was set up in 1928. Led by architect and urban planner Cornelis van Eesteren (1897-1988) and Jakoba Mulder (1900-1988), the Algemeen Uitbreidingsplan (General Expansion Plan, or AUP) was drawn up in 1935, in which new urban and architectural ideas of 'light, air and space' were central. Because of the Second World War, construction did not begin until the early

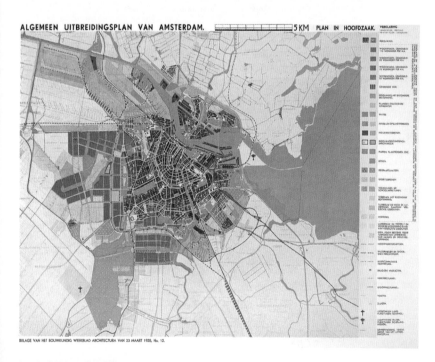

General Expansion Plan, 1935.

1950s, with garden city Slotermeer  as the first result. After the Western Garden Cities and, to the south, Buitenveldert, Amsterdam North also saw a major expansion after the construction of the IJ-tunnel 33. From 1966, Amsterdam gained another large-scale new neighbourhood to the east: the Bijlmermeer 95. This 'model suburb' with 40,000 homes for 'modern people' was characterized by large-scale high-rise buildings and a completely autonomous infrastructure.

The clearance of the Nieuwmarkt district during the construction of the metro in 1977.

In response to the 'city thinking' of the time, from the 1960s onwards, local residents rose up against the city council's large-scale plans and demolition plans for the city centre. Amsterdam became the stronghold of the squatting movement, in which young people looking for a place to live moved into empty buildings. The dilapidation of the Nieuwmarkt district reached its peak around 1970, when large-scale interventions such as the construction of a metro 75 and thoroughfares 78 were prepared. After an emotionally charged conflict, the importance of urban renewal was acknowledged and the reconstruction of the Nieuwmarkt district 7 was adapted to existing building lines and scale.

Also because of the growing appreciation for the preservation of historical heritage, the city developed vacant port and industrial areas into new residential areas from the 1990s onwards, such as in the Eastern Docklands, with the Eastern Quay 86, Java Island 87, KNSM Island 88 and Borneo-Sporenburg 89. This urban planning series was continued with IJburg 98, a series of artificial islands further east in the IJ Lake. Amsterdam will continue to develop in the future, this time westwards, with the new Haven-Stad ('Port-City') residential area estimated to have between 40,000 and 70,000 new homes.

Burgemeester Vening Meineszlaan,
Burgemeester van Tienhovengracht,
Burgemeester Eliasstraat
C. van Eesteren
1935-1955

With 10,000 homes, garden city Slotermeer is the largest early post-war residential district in the Netherlands. The neighbourhood was designed based on the 1935 General Extension Plan for Amsterdam by architect and urban planner Cornelis van Eesteren (1897-1988). With an open design of mainly low-rise buildings in rows with lots of greenery in between, the ideal residential district was realized according to the ideas of the Congrès Internationaux d'Architecture Moderne (CIAM). The innovative urban design ideas of the CIAM, which Van Eesteren chaired between 1930 and 1947, broke with the traditional closed building block with continuous street walls applied by H.P. Berlage in his Plan Zuid 🔢. It was not until 1951 that the first pile was driven for this garden city. A large part of Slotermeer, between Burgemeester Vening Meineszlaan, the railway line to the east, Burgemeester van Tienhovengracht and Burgemeester Eliasstraat, was designated a protected cityscape in 2007 under the name Van Eesteren Outdoor Museum.

Van Eesteren Pavilion   🏛

The Van Eesteren Pavilion on Sloterplas (Noordzijde 31), a transparent design by Korteknie Stuhlmacher Architects, has housed the Van Eesteren Indoor Museum, an information centre about the Western Garden Cities, since 2017. From here, excursions are organized and it is possible to visit a 1952 museum house that has been completely restored to its original 1950s state with a coal stove, Bakelite telephone and Bruynzeel kitchen (Freek Oxstraat 27).

Comeniusstraat and environs
J.F. Berghoef
1955-1960
J.G. Goeting (art)

To reduce the housing shortage, modular construction was introduced after the Second World War, enabling cheap and fast construction. Various building systems with prefabricated components have been used, including Dura-Coignet, Brick Montage Building, the Pronto system and the originally British Airey system. Some 8,500 Nemavo-Airey homes have been built in the Netherlands, almost half of them in Amsterdam. Low-rise as in the Jeruzalem neighbourhood in Watergraafsmeer, but also multi-storey buildings, such as this complex with thirteen four-storey porch flats, three seven-storey high-rise blocks, a twelve-storey tower block and a block of studio apartments. It also includes petrol stations, garages and some retail blocks. Characteristic are the taller blocks of maisonettes built over an ornamental canal and fitted with emergency spiral staircases. It is curious that architect Johannes Berghoef (1903-1994), one of the forerunners of the very traditionally oriented Delft School, had the licence for this construction system.

Miss Mulder

MSc Jakoba Mulder (1900-1988) worked from 1930 as one of the few women in the Urban Development division of the Public Works Department led by Cornelis van Eesteren. She designed the Amsterdam Forest and was one of the driving forces behind the development of the 1935 General Extension Plan. On her initiative, a large number of public children's playgrounds 25 59 were realized from 1947 onwards, mainly designed by architect Aldo van Eyck. In 1958, she succeeded Cornelis van Eesteren as head of the Urban Development division.

47 St Joseph Church

Erik de Roodestraat 14-16
G.H.M. Holt, K.P. Tholens
1941-1952
M. de Leeuw (art)

Catholic architect Gerard Holt (1904-1988) played an important role in the change in church construction after the Second World War. Undignified materials such as concrete and steel were no longer taboo, costly ornamentation could be omitted and a church building did not need a display of power. St Joseph's Church has a basilica shape and could accommodate 1130 people. The concrete structure is partly left in sight in the interior and exterior. The facades consist of Limburg natural stone and concrete slabs, while the flat roof is made of prefabricated concrete elements. With the Catholic schools, a convent for the teachers and a few rows of now demolished houses for the elderly, there was a small Catholic enclave here. In 1990, the church was closed and, after a period of vacancy, put to use as a climbing hall. Since 2016, Candy Castle play paradise has been located here.

Modern Churches

After the Second World War, there was a revolution in church architecture. Inspired among other things by Le Corbusier's 1955 chapel in Ronchamp, architects experimented with modern materials, the layout of the liturgical centre and the position of the church tower. Well-known modern churches in Amsterdam are the 1955 Roman Catholic Church of the Resurrection (Kolenkit) by Marius Duintjer (Bos en Lommerplein 327) and the 1966 Dutch Reformed Thomas Church by Karel Sijmons (Prinses Irenestraat 36).

48   Westermoskee

Piri Reïsplein
Breitman & Breitman
1994-2015

The Westermoskee (Western Mosque) was designed by French-Jewish architect couple Marc (1949) and Nada Breitman (1952). In total, it took 22 years before the building was finally completed. The design was inspired by the Aya Sofia in Istanbul, but executed in Dutch brick, white woodwork and detailing in the style of the Amsterdam School. The minaret is 42 metres tall. The large dome is 25 metres in diameter; there are also seven and nine smaller domes on the side walls and four half-domes at the corners. 1,700 Muslims can pray there. The mosque is at the centre of a square, of which the sides were also designed by the architect couple. There is a car park under the square. The Hotel Not Hotel has a quaint interior with rooms in an old tram carriage and mysterious book rooms.

Instagrammable Architecture

With the rise of social media and the ubiquitous availability of a camera on mobile phones, the city and architecture are valued differently. A building must be suitable for a selfie for Instagram or TikTok. Highly photogenic are architect Sjoerd Soeters' Pyramids, a 50-metre-high residential complex on Jan van Galenstraat built in 2006.

Ookmeerweg/Reimerswaalstraat
MVRDV
1994-1997

As part of a comprehensive densification operation in the Western
Garden Cities, the architectural firm
MVRDV used the building guidelines
from Cornelis van Eesteren's General
Extension Plan as a starting point for
this stacked residential care complex
(WoZoCo) with a hundred homes for
the elderly. As only 87 dwellings could
fit on the site within these urban planning preconditions, the remaining
thirteen dwellings were combined

into five separate blocks and hung
from the glass gallery side of the
block. The sight of the 11-metre can-
tilevered blocks looks equally frivo-
lous and alienating in the streetscape
of Ookmeerweg. Because the blocks
are as deep as the gallery flat itself and
they are not supported, they appear
to defy gravity. Like the rear facade,
the five differently designed blocks
have horizontal wooden cladding of
red cedar. The rear facade features a
series of cheerful Plexiglas balconies
in purple, yellow, orange and green.

The Steelman

As part of the urban renewal in the
Staalman neighbourhood, artist
Florentijn Hofman (1977) designed this
giant bear with a pillow under his arm.
Hofman developed the ten-metre-high
bear made of sprayed concrete and steel in
consultation with young people from the
neighbourhood. The Steelman on Ottho
Heldringstraat radiates self-confidence
because of his sturdy appearance, but
with the pillow under his arm he also has
a soft side.

50 Suspension Bridge Maisonnettes

Dijkgraafplein
J.P. Kloos
1964-1970

The idea for the remarkable layout of this complex came from a 1962 competition for experimental housing, won by architect Jan Piet Kloos (1905-2001). There are 232 maisonettes and also shops on the ground floor, garages in the basement and an intermediate layer of 15 single-storey flats. The bedroom floors of the maisonettes are sometimes upstairs, sometimes downstairs. This way, the number of galleries could be limited to one per four floors. From the gallery, half-storey steps always lead up or down to four linked entrances. The galleries are made of steel and suspended in front of the residential blocks; thus, they take away less light. They hang from an extra-weighted concrete canopy above the entrances; the sloping lines in the suspension coincide with the stairs. Making the galleries slightly wider than usual created a raised street for neighbourly contact and for children to play.

Bicycle City

The Netherlands is cycling country par excellence and for a historic city like Amsterdam, the bicycle is the ideal means of transport. Forty per cent of traffic is made up of cyclists, and the municipality has built a great number of parking facilities for them. Quite spectacular are wUrck's two underground bicycle parking facilities at Central Station **1** for a total of 11,000 bicycles. At the rear side of the station, in the IJ, there is another parking for 4,000 bicycles by VenhoevenCS. Under Leidseplein **23** is a parking for 200 bicycles by architectural studio ZJA.

51   Olympic Stadium ▣ ⵏ ⊨ Ⓗ

Olympisch Stadion 2
J. Wils
1926-1928
C. van Eesteren, G. Jonkheid (ass.);
G.J.W. Rueb (art); A.J. van Stigt (rest.)

This stadium was built for the 1928 Olympics in Amsterdam. Architect Jan Wils (1891-1972) was well connected in the sports world and designed an elliptical stadium with stands all around. The stands rest on a concrete supporting structure, but the facades are made of brick. The roof is supported by steel truss girders. The slender, 46-metre-high Marathon Tower, the carrier of the Olympic Flame, marks the main entrance. The lighting of the Olympic Flame was Wils' idea, and has remained part of the opening ceremony in subsequent Olympics ever since. For his design, Wils was awarded a gold Olympic medal for architecture. After serving as a football stadium for many years, the building was to be demolished in the early 1990s to make way for housing development. After fierce protests, the stadium was saved, renovated and taken into use as an athletics stadium. In the process, a concrete second ring that was added later was removed. The stadium now houses a café-restaurant, a conference centre, gyms and business premises.

Olympic Salute

Prominently placed next to the Marathon Tower was the Van Tuyll monument from 1928 in memory of this founder of the Dutch Olympic Committee. An athlete gives the Olympic salute, which bears a strong resemblance to the Nazi salute. In 2020, the statue by sculptor Gra Rueb (1885-1972) was therefore moved to the stairwell. On the forecourt, in memory of athletes killed in the Second World War, there is the sculpture Prometheus by Fred Carasso. Behind the stadium is a remarkable statue of the first minute of the 1974 World Cup final, which ended dramatically for the Dutch fans, with Berti

Vogts tackling Johan Cruijff inside the penalty box. It was created by sculptor Ek van Zanten.

52   Gerrit Rietveld Academy

Frederik Roeskestraat 96
Rietveld Van Dillen Van Tricht
1959-1967
Benthem Crouwel (exp. 2000-2004),
Studio Fedlev (exp. 2012-2018)

Founded in 1924, this university of applied sciences for fine arts and design consists of three buildings. The main building by architect Gerrit Rietveld (1888-1964) is characterized by the use of a 'rhythmic concrete skeleton', which allowed a flexible layout of the school building. In Arnhem, the architect realized a similar building almost simultaneously. By placing the facade at a distance of forty centimetres from the floors, the glass facades extend to the roof without interruption, creating an all-glass box. Glass is also used extensively in the interior. In 2004, the Rietveld building was renovated and complemented by Benthem Crouwel with a second building. The facades of the 9-storey Benthem-Crouwel building are also made of glass: small square ribbed glass panels on three sides and plain glass on the fourth – the north facade that is so important to artists. The third building, by Fedlev, was completed in 2018 and is also characterized by a high degree of transparency. The 'open' building features a roof terrace and has entrances on all sides. When the weather is good, the facades can be opened and the outdoor space can be used as an additional maker space.

Spring-cleaning

With his graduation project at the Gerrit Rietveld Academy in 1992, artist Job Koelewijn (1962) already attracted international attention with a performance. In it, he had his mother and three aunts, all dressed in the traditional costume of his native village of Spakenburg, clean the Rietveld building. This was an homage to the clear visual language of architect Gerrit Rietveld and a reckoning with his student days.

53 Burgerweeshuis

IJsbaanpad 3
A.E. van Eyck
1955-1960
WDJ Architects (ren. 2016-2018)

With the Burgerweeshuis (Amsterdam Orphanage), designed in 1955 by architect Aldo van Eyck (1918-1999) to house 125 orphans, the architect aimed to bring back the human scale and individuality in architecture. Constructed as a labyrinth of pavilions in a complex configuration around patios, the orphanage became the first built manifesto of Structuralism in Dutch architecture.

The complex is composed of linked standard modules with domed reinforced concrete roof elements on a grid of 3.36 x 3.36 metres. Within this system, the different spaces vary, from communal inner streets to more private individual rooms. A configuration of a number of rooms together with a larger square space forms a ward, marked by a larger dome. The building had eight of these children's wards for different age groups. The older groups had a sleeping floor and an open outdoor space; the younger groups had

an enclosed outdoor space (patio). By blending the private and collective, the architect created a sheltered environment for each individual child. In the interiors, many surprising effects were achieved with level differences, intermediate spaces, circular, sunken or raised sections and a diagonal focus of attention and activities. The different wards were connected by an inner street with the same rough materials as the exterior and lit with street lamps. In addition to the connected wards, the building contained larger halls for recreation and sports, a central kitchen, an infirmary, an administration area and some staff residences. The latter were located on the first floor, forming an elongated, natural canopy of the entrance area.

The interior of the building has since been altered several times. In 1986, major conversion plans were drawn up for the complex, including partial demolition. After an international campaign, the complex was preserved and the new Tripolis office complex **54** was developed next door, under the direction of the architect couple Aldo and Hannie van Eyck. After a new restoration led by architect Wessel de Jonge

(1957), the Burgerweeshuis has been the headquarters of a project developer since 2018.

Burgerweeshuispad 101
A.E. & H. van Eyck
1990-1994
MVRDV (exp. 2018-2023)

On a site next to the Burgerweeshuis 53 of his design, architect Aldo van Eyck (1918-1999) and his wife Hannie van Eyck-van Roojen (1918-2008) created three monumental office blocks, thirty years later. The use of materials (untreated wood for the facade) and the colours (rainbow) are characteristic of these architects' later works. The structure of the octagonal blocks, rising in height, is the same: a central tower with the entrance, traffic areas and sanitary facilities linking three office wings each. The polygonal office spaces are arranged in an open, non-hierarchical manner and can be subdivided by means of movable partitions. The office complex was re-developed in 2023 with an extension by architectural firm MVRDV. To protect the old complex (and save it from demolition), they designed a horizontal 'groundscraper' as a sound barrier next to the busy A10 South ring road. The two buildings flow into each other with stairs and bridges in what the architects say is a surprising 'symbiosis of old and new'.

One of the existing Tripolis blocks has been transformed into a residential building with social housing flats.

55 ING House

Amstelveenseweg 500/Skûtsjespad
Meyer & Van Schooten
1998-2002

Banking and financial services corporation ING wanted an innovative office building in a high-profile location along the motorway. The distinctive main form, a design by Roberto Meyer (1959) and Jeroen van Schooten (1960), was inspired by the streamlined shapes of fast-moving traffic. By placing the building on legs, all offices have views over the surrounding area. There is a glass entrance area between the legs. In the interior, a high degree of openness has been created through the lavish use of glass walls, atria, courtyard gardens and loggias. The facades are also largely made of glass, to reflect its openness and transparency. By using two layers of glass, natural ventilation is possible without noise nuisance from the motorway. The auditorium in the tip has aluminium cladding and a window overlooking the green surroundings. After twelve years, ING left the premises for cheaper offices and the building, nicknamed 'the dust-buster', was renamed Infinity.

VU Amsterdam

Amsterdam has two universities, the University of Amsterdam (UvA), concentrated near Roeterseiland, and the Vrije Universiteit ('Free University', VU) in Buitenveldert. VU was founded in 1879 and has a Protestant-Christian signature. VU's buildings are brutalist, especially the 1973 main building (De Boelelaan 1105) by Architectengroep 69. With sixteen floors and 90,000 square metres of floor area, it was one of the tallest and largest buildings in the city. In 2009, there were plans to demolish it, leading to protests among students and architects.

🍽 🛏

Gustav Mahlerlaan and environs
P.B. de Bruijn i.c.w. various architects
1995-2030

On a strip about one kilometre wide and 3.5 kilometres long along the A10 ring road and the southern railway line, a business district has sprung up since 1998, based on an urban design by architect Pi de Bruijn (1942). Ideally located between Schiphol Airport and the old city centre, with a university, the World Trade Centre, good public transport facilities such as Station Zuid 75 and the RAI convention centre 67 nearby. Besides more than a million square metres of office space, 7,000 homes and a variety of facilities

for users and residents are planned. In the area, the motorway will be in a tunnel; train and metro will remain above ground. After a hesitant start, partly due to the property crisis, construction of both office buildings and residential buildings has been in full swing since 2017. A host of national and international architects have been brought in for this.

List of buildings Zuidas

Beethovenstraat 503
MVRDV
2015-2022
P. Oudolf (landscaping)

One of the landmarks of the Zuidas 56 is this extraordinary complex by MVRDV, the architectural firm of Winy Maas (1959), Jacob van Rijs (1965) and Nathalie de Vries (1965). The complex contains a combination of commercial functions in the substructure, office space on the seven layers above, and residential units in three towers of 67, 81 and 100 metres high. There is an underground car park and bicycle parking. The 198 apartments, all with unique floor plans, have a rock-like facade of natural stone on the inside. The mirror-glass facade on the outside complements the surrounding office buildings. The terraces and balconies were designed in collaboration with landscape architect Piet Oudolf (1944) and planted with plants and shrubs that are wind-resistant and can thrive at high altitudes. On the fourth floor is the semi-public 'valley', accessible via a public route. Running through the building is the 'grotto', an indoor shopping street.

High-rises

The 40-metre-high Wolkenkrabber, also called the 12-Storey House or Skyscraper 64 at Victorieplein in 1932 was one of the first high-rise housing projects in the Netherlands. There was no room for high-rise buildings in the historic centre, and because of the failed Bijlmermeer 95, high-rises had a bad reputation in Amsterdam for a long time. In the late 1980s, the lack of space necessitated new ones, though. At 135 metres, ZZ&P's Rembrandt Tower has been the tallest since 1995. On the Zuidas 56, office buildings reach around

100 metres. High-rise buildings are also being built on the banks of the IJ 39, a good location for residential towers.

The Amsterdam School

The Amsterdam School is the name of an architectural style that originated in Amsterdam around the time of the First World War and whose projects are mainly found in Amsterdam. The style is in line with international, especially German, expressionism. Due to the war, few buildings were built in Europe, but this style did emerge in the Netherlands, which was neutral. Features are expressive, distinctive applications of otherwise traditional materials such as brick, wood, roof tiles and natural stone combined with special decorations and fine art. Architect Michel de Klerk's Hillehuis at Johannes Vermeerplein 34, built in 1912, is considered the first example. The projects for Eigen Haard in the Spaarndammerbuurt 40 and De Dageraad in Amsterdam South 69 are highlights of housing association architecture. The striking Shipping House 3 by Johan Melchior van der Meij is the most famous building. The name of this movement was coined in 1916 by architect and publicist Jan Gratama. The magazine *Wendingen* edited by H.Th. Wijdeveld was its main mouthpiece.

The Amsterdam School took off in the interwar period when the new districts Plan Zuid 63 and Plan West 44 were built. The aesthetics committee prescribed Amsterdam School architecture here. Because often only the facades were designed by the Amsterdam School architects and the floor plans by the contractor, the movement has been accused of being 'pinafore architecture'. Its opponents, including the functionalists of the Nieuwe Bouwen movement, felt that the architects of the Amsterdam School paid far too little attention to good, practical and healthy housing. But the Public Works Department of the municipality of Amsterdam embraced the Amsterdam School and many hundreds of schools, bridges 58 and police stations as well as street furniture 40 were designed in this style.

Contrary to what the name suggests, Amsterdam School architecture can also be found outside Amsterdam. The architects of the Government Buildings Agency built many buildings in this style. Architect Joseph Crouwel (1885-1962), for instance, who designed the main post office and university buildings in Utrecht, and Cornelis Blaauw (1885-1947), designer of many university buildings in Wageningen. Many architects of local Municipal Services also realized school buildings and other municipal buildings in this style. A separate variant of the Amsterdam School even emerged in Groningen, with a more geometric style by architects such as Egbert Reitsma and Evert van Linge.

In the artists' village of Bergen in North Holland, five architects were given a free hand in 1917 to design villas in Park Meerwijk. This overall project of detached houses is known as one of the highlights of the Amsterdam School outside the city of Amsterdam.

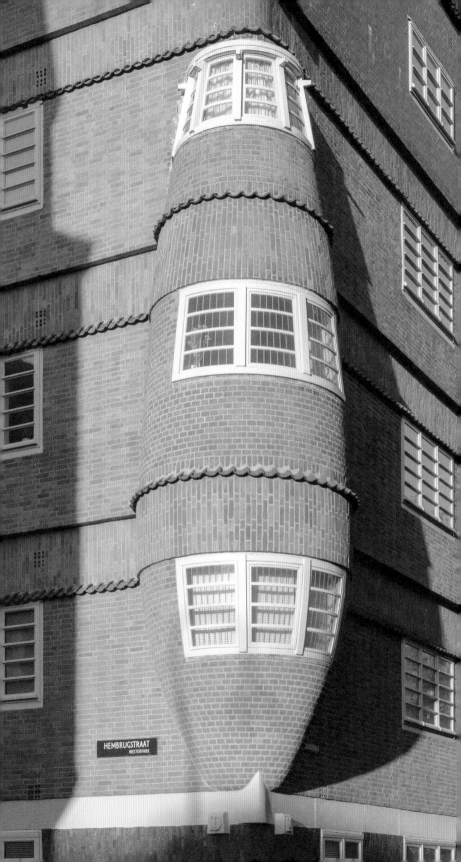

58 Bridge and Boathouse

Olympiaplein
P.L. Kramer
1926-1928
H.L. Krop (art)

The 1928 Lyceum Bridge by bridge builder Pieter Lodewijk Kramer (1881-1961) is part of an axis in the urban plan for Amsterdam-South 53, starting at one square (Olympiaplein) and ending at another (Valeriusplein). Here, two former semi-underground 'privy houses' from 1922, a men's toilet *and* a ladies' toilet, by architect Jan de Meijer (1878-1950) have been converted into commercial spaces. The fixed bridge over the canal Noorder Amstelkanaal has jetties for the rowing boats of the students of the

Amsterdam Lyceum, which is built with arches over the axis. There are two small bridge houses with vaulted roofs: a boatman's house with sleeping accommodation and a house with a toilet. Beautifully symmetrical here is the Indies-Netherlands Monument, originally the Van Heutsz Memorial, designed by architect Gijsbert Friedhoff in collaboration with sculptor Frits van Hall. The monument consists of an 18-metre-high memorial column with a female figure in front of it holding a scroll of the law, flanked by two lions and several reliefs. A pond and a wall surround it. This tribute to this brutal governor of Aceh in the former Dutch East Indies, was highly controversial even at its unveiling in 1935.

The Pee Curl

Initially, public urinals in Amsterdam were built over the canals. Around 1880, the Public Works Department designed a new type: a spiral-shaped steel sheet on four iron legs around an upright natural-stone slab. The transparency allows police to check if there is more than one person in the 'curl', as the urinal is named after its shape. There are still 35 restored pee curls in the city centre. One specimen has been moved to the Open Air Museum in Arnhem.

📖 ¶|

Vondelpark
J.D. Zocher jr., L.P. Zocher
1864-1865/1878

By selling plots of land in the area, a group of wealthy and prominent Amsterdam residents was able to fund this elongated 'park for riding and strolling' in 1865. Garden architects Jan David Zocher Jr (1791-1870) and his son Louis Paul Zocher (1820-1915) designed Vondelpark in a romantic English garden style with winding paths, wavy water features and elegant bridges. The bandstand from 1873 was also designed by them. The entire park was laid out in a number of different phases over a period of fourteen years. The various buildings in Vondelpark were also financed privately, such as the monumental Renaissance-style Vondelpark Pavilion (W. Hamer, 1879-1881) and the modernist tearoom 't Blauwe Theehuis (H.A.J. & J. Baanders, 1936). A bridge was built across Vondelpark in later years (P.L. Kramer, 1947). Near the Kattenlaantje is a water playground with a number of sand-boxes and climbing frames, designed by Aldo van Eyck. The Vondelpark remained in private ownership until 1953. Since then, it has been public and Amsterdam's most visited city park.

Summer of Love

The hippie era also left its mark on Vondelpark. In the late 1960s, young people from all over the world flocked to the 'magic centre' of Amsterdam to sleep, play music and smoke cannabis together in the Vondelpark. With a flower in their hair, a necklace with the ban-the-bomb sign and so-called 'love-ins', hippies opposed war and violence and celebrated love and freedom.

Willem Witsenstraat 12, 14
H. Hertzberger
1980-1983

Because of their prominent location in a high-end residential area, the Willemsparkschool and the Montessori school were designed as detached volumes. Both schools have the kindergarten classrooms on the ground floor and outdoor classrooms on the second floor. With these schools, architect Herman Hertzberger (1932) introduced a new concept in school building: by concentrating the traffic space in the heart of the school, adding a skylight and designing the stairs as a kind of amphitheatre, a central activity space was created within the margins of the tight budget and programme of requirements for schools. The schools have a concrete core, filled in with B2 blocks, Hertzberger's favourite building material, and feature a variety of steel additions. The architecture is inspired by architect Jan Duiker's Open Air School **62**.

Hilton Hotel

In June 1969, newlyweds John Lennon and Yoko Ono moved into the bridal suite of the Hilton Hotel to stay in bed for a week. Apart from a lot of publicity, this Bed-in for Peace also evoked much scepticism. In *The Ballad Of John And Yoko* Lennon himself described it like this:

Drove from Paris to the Amsterdam Hilton,
Talking in our beds for a week,
The newspapers said, 'Say what you doing in bed?',
I said, 'We're only trying to get us some peace'.

Anthonie van Dijckstraat 4-12
W. van Tijen, M.A. Stam, C.I.A. Stam-Beese, H.A. Maaskant
1935-1936

These five drive-in houses might well be the first houses of this later widely used type in the Netherlands. Those who could afford a car and a garage also needed a sizeable house. The first floor contains a generous living room, dining room and kitchen. An external staircase provides direct access to the garden. The two floors above contain the master bedroom, three children's bedrooms, a bathroom with bath, a guest room and a servant's quarters.

There is a sizeable balcony. At the rear, the roof is pitched. With the large windows, balconies and flower boxes in front and above the entrance, a city house was created with optimal 'associations with sun, greenery and openness'. Architect Willem van Tijen (1894-1974) left most of the design to Mart Stam (1899-1986) and his wife Lotte Stam-Beese (1903-1988), who had returned from the Soviet Union and had little work.

Montessori School

Next to the houses is a second building by architect Van Tijen, the Montessori school (entrance Albrecht Dürerstraat 36). Van Tijen was so impressed by the Open Air School 62 that he offered architect Jan Duiker the commission. Duiker declined and did not want to work on it with him either. In 1936, the plan was ready. Although Van Tijen was afraid of the aesthetics committee, he succeeded in creating a bright modern building with a lot of glass and large balconies between the surrounding brick blocks. Between school and gymnasium is the playground with a garden.

62 Openluchtschool

Cliostraat 40
J. Duiker, B. Bijvoet
1927-1930

Open-air schools were built from the beginning of the last century to allow frail children to recover in the sun and the open air. In 1927, architects Jan Duiker (1890-1935) and Bernard Bijvoet (1889-1979) were commissioned to design an Openluchtschool voor het Gezonde Kind (Open Air School for the Healthy Child) in Amsterdam South. The school was built on a court-yard of a closed building block, as there was no place for a modern func-tional design in the Amsterdam School architecture of Plan Zuid 63. In the Openluchtschool, the ideals of modern architecture – light, air and space – were demonstratively manifested. The school ranks with Duikers Zonnestraal ('Ray of sun') in Hilversum (1931) and Brinkman & Van der Vlugt's Van Nelle Factory in Rotterdam (1931) among the highlights of New Building in the Netherlands.
The school consists of a four-storey square block of classrooms placed diagonally on the site. The basic square is divided into four quadrants around a diagonally placed central stairwell. The east and west quadrants

each contain one classroom per floor and share a south-facing open-air classroom. The north quadrant is built on the ground floor only and contains a staff room. The ground floor also con-tains a classroom in the west quadrant, the main entrance under the open-air classrooms and an elongated, recessed gymnasium that is pushed halfway under the classroom block because of its greater height.
The concrete columns are not placed at the corners but in the middle of the quadrant sides. This leaves the cor-ners column-free and accentuates the open, floating character of the school. The floor slabs cantilever over the facade beams, producing a favour-able distribution of forces. The col-umns and beams are narrower at the

top and towards the ends, respectively, demonstrating the distribution of forces in the structure. Apart from a low concrete parapet, the facades are entirely glazed and fitted with steel-framed pivot windows, allowing the classrooms to be opened up entirely. At the bottom of the concrete floors, heating pipes were poured along with the concrete. This system of heating from the ceiling down, chosen so as to be able to open the windows in winter, was only moderately successful and was replaced in 1955. Characteristic of Duiker's careful attention to detail are the coat pegs. These are attached to the heating pipes in the hall, which simultaneously heat the hall and dry the coats.

The gateway building on Cliostraat consists of a housing block to the right of the gateway and a handicrafts room above the bicycle storage and entrance. The relatively low and transparent building allows a good view of the school from the street.

In 1940, headmaster Piet Bakkum and Johannes Röntgen wrote the school anthem:

Open air school, open-air school
With your classes light and bright.
With your windows swinging open
to the side with much sunlight.
Open air school, open-air school,
with your classes near the sky.
With your gymnastics and crafts
and things to learn and try.
Here I like to go to school,
Here I am both serious and a fool.

63 Plan Zuid ☕ 🍴

Vrijheidslaan, Minervalaan and environs ▽
H.P. Berlage
1915-1917/1940

Following an earlier plan from 1900, architect Hendrik Petrus Berlage (1856-1934) presented his final design for an urban development plan for Amsterdam South fifteen years later. Plan Zuid ('South Plan') is based on geometric patterns (pentagons) with two main axes: the Vrijheidslaan from the new bridge over the Amstel (H.P. Berlage, 1926-1932) to Victorieplein with J.F. Staal's Wolkenkrabber 64, and the monumental axis across

Minervalaan (architects: C.J. Blaauw, G.J. Rutgers and J.F. Berghoef), that was to lead up to a future and never realized Zuiderstation ('South station') here. With his emphasis on the building block with closed street walls, Berlage created a plan layout that is a synthesis between the collective and the monumental. When the plan was implemented between 1925 and 1940, the architects of the Amsterdam School in particular were favoured to use their sculptural style to create an exuberant mix of sculptural facades, imaginative brickwork, wavy rooflines and expressively shaped window frames.

Pinafore Architecture

Architect Michel de Klerk (1884-1923) only designed the facades for his building block at Vrijheidslaan 10-54. This was not unusual at the time and is probably one of the reasons why expressions of the Amsterdam School are often called 'schortjesarchitectuur' ('pinafore architecture'). De Klerk's facade is characterized by round bay windows with staggered balconies creating diagonally stepped lines. For the building on the other side of the road, Piet Kramer designed the facade.

64   De Wolkenkrabber

Victorieplein 45-47
J.F. Staal
1927-1932

At the point where three wide traffic boulevards converge in the Berlage-designed Plan Zuid 63, architect Jan Frederik Staal (1879-1940) designed this modern, monumental residential tower. The 40-metre-high Wolkenkrabber (Skyscraper), also called the 12-Storey House, towers well above the surrounding residential blocks. The tower was one of the first high-rise residential projects in the Netherlands. Staal used modern materials such as steel, glass and concrete for the building, but chose the more traditional yellow brick for the facades. The Wolkenkrabber thus shows characteristics of both the Amsterdam School and functionalism. The symmetrical tower has a lift in the centre and a stairwell with six-room flats on either side. Shops are located on the lower floors. The Wolkenkrabber was completed in 1932 with many 'modern' conveniences, including a porter, rubbish chutes, lift, central heating, hot water, speaking tubes and electric doorbells.

Berlage

In front of the building is an imposing statue of architect Hendrik Petrus Berlage (1856-1934), the designer of Plan Zuid 63. The 6-metre-high Belgian bluestone statue was carved by city sculptor Hildo Krop (1884-1970), who worked on it for ten years. It was placed in 1966 and shows the architect Berlage looking out towards the Berlage Bridge he designed at the end of Vrijheidslaan.

65 Synagogue

Lekstraat 61
A. Elzas
1934-1937

Young architect Abraham Elzas (1907-1995) won a closed competition among nine Jewish architects for a synagogue in Amsterdam-South. The business-like design raised some eyebrows and initially received much criticism: it was said to resemble a bulb shed or warehouse rather than a monumental house of worship. Elzas designed a rectangular main building with the long axis facing southeast. On the ground floor was the hall for men, on the first floor the gallery for women. An annex contained meeting rooms, an extra synagogue and an administrator's house. The men's cloakroom formed a connecting corridor. The synagogue is clad in slabs of natural stone and has an interior of white and dark red marble. The annex is made of brick. On the facade is the Hebrew text: 'And I will dwell among the children of Israel, and will not forsake my people Israel.' (1 Kings 6:13). An auction house has been located in the building since 1999.

De Bijenkorf

After the Second World War, architect Abraham Elzas worked for the Bijenkorf ('Beehive'), a department store with a Jewish signature. He was involved in the design for the Rotterdam store by American architect Marcel Breuer and designed many HEMA department stores. Simon Philip Goudsmit started the Bijenkorf in 1870 as a small haberdashery shop at Nieuwendijk 132. The large department store on Damrak by architect Jacques van Straaten Jr opened in 1913.

66   Studio Apartments

Zomerdijkstraat 16-30
Zanstra, Giesen, Sijmons
1932-1934

The complex of 32 studio apartments was built in 1934 at the initiative and design of the then young architects Piet Zanstra (1905-2003), Jan Giesen (1903-1980) and Karel Sijmons (1908-1989). It was the first project of their joint firm. The striking difference between the two long facades of this block is explained by its function: the building provides both living and working spaces for visual artists. On the north side, with its favourable light, the studios with high glass windows are spread over four floors; the south side with its balconies contains the various living areas and has six floors. With the difference in height between the living units and the studios, the architects enabled alternating small (one storey) and larger dwellings (two storeys). Stairs connect the living units and studios. The expanded ground floor was specially designed for sculptors; above it were the painters' studios. Well-known artists such as Jan Wolkers, Charlotte van Pallandt and Fred Carasso lived in the complex.

Turks Fruit

Writer/sculptor Jan Wolkers (1925-2007) is standing here with actors Rutger Hauer (1944-2019) and Monique van de Ven (1952) in front of his studio on the Uiterwaardenstraat side of the block of studio apartments. His explicit love novel *Turks Fruit* ('Turkish Delight') was made into a film in 1973 by director Paul Verhoeven with both young actors in the lead roles. *Turks Fruit* is the most successful film in Dutch cinema of all time with 3.3 million visitors.

Europaplein 24
A. Bodon (DSBV)/Benthem Crouwel
1951-1961

The event, conference and exhibition complex of the RAI (acronym for Rijwiel en Automobiel Industrie) was constructed in several phases. The first exhibition building on this site is the characteristic, curved Europa Hall from 1961, designed by architect Alexander Bodon (1906-1993). With its open end walls and large skylights, the strikingly bright hall has impressive dimensions; 67.5 by 195 metres with a clear height of 16.5 metres. The span consists of thin steel arched trusses resting on heavy concrete supports. As supervisor of the RAI complex, in addition to the Europa Hall (1951-1961) Bodon also designed the Congress Centre (1961-1965) and the Amstel Hall (1969 with extension 1977-1982). From 1989, architectural firm Benthem Crouwel took over this role. Among other things, they designed the stainless steel Elicium (2005-2009) with its large overhanging canopy above the complex's new entrance, the sustainable Amtrium (2011-2015) with a vertical greenhouse, and a new multi-functional, 30-metre-high parking building (2014-2016), which appears to be inspired by architect Piet Zanstra's Europarking **37**, built in 1971.

Advertising Column

The RAI's 42-metre-high advertising column, an expressive design by graphic designer Dick Elffers (1910-1990) from 1961, has now been listed as a National Monument along with the Europa Hall. Reportedly, Reinier de Graaf and Rem Koolhaas of the architecture firm OMA were so inspired by the distinctive triangular shape of this column that they used it as the basis for their design with twisted triangular volumes of the nearby nhow hotel (2016-2020).

68 Zorgvlied

Amsteldijk 273
J.D. Zocher jr., L.P. Zocher
1867-1869

The oldest, Roman Catholic part of Zorgvlied cemetery was designed by garden architect Johan David Zocher Jr. (1791-1870) in the English garden style. There was a first extension as early as 1892, a second in 1900 and further extensions in 1919 and 1926. An auditorium was added in 1931. There were also several extensions after the Second World War, so that the cemetery now totals 16 hectares. A modern auditorium designed by Claus & Kaan was added in 1998 and the Crematorion by Group A in 2016. There is an information column in the hall of the office, where visitors can search for a grave.

Graves

Many local celebrities are buried at Zorgvlied, such as pop stars Herman Brood with a large angel on his grave and Bobby Farrell (from Boney M.), authors Harry Mulisch and Annie M.G. Schmidt, and Kerwin Duinmeyer, victim of a racist murder. Architects are also buried here: Eduard Cuypers, Jan Duiker, Ernst van der Pek and city sculptor Hildo Krop, with the funerary monument De Eeuwige Vrouw ('The Eternal Woman'). Notable funerary monuments include those for circus entrepreneur Oscar Carré (1891) **77**, the Dorrepaal family (1886) and the weeping angel for P. vom Rath-Bunge (1894), all national monuments. And the guardian gorilla on the grave of criminal Jules Jie.

69 De Dageraad

Pieter Lodewijk Takstraat and environs ▽
M. de Klerk, P.L. Kramer
1919-1922
H.L. Krop, J.A. Rädecker (art)

These workers' houses for the socialist housing association De Dageraad ('The Dawn') were designed by the two main exponents of the Amsterdam School: Michel de Klerk (1884-1923) and Piet Kramer (1881-1961). While Amsterdam School architects were often called in to embellish the facades of standard residential blocks, in this case De Klerk and Kramer also designed the floor plans. The houses were built with municipal subsidy and comply with the building regulations (maximum four storeys, stairwells in direct connection with the outside air, maximum volume of living space, and so on). The complex contains mostly three- and four-bedroom apartments, which meant a significant improvement in living situation for the workers who became residents there. The fact that, in addition to spacious houses, considerable attention could also and above all be paid to the exterior is mainly due to the constant efforts by socialist councillor Floor Wibaut to defend against criticism about the alleged profligacy and unnecessary embellishment of the street walls. Indeed, his bust is incorporated into one of the street corners of the complex.
De Klerk's work mainly concerns the houses at Thérèse Schwartzeplein and Henriette Ronnerplein. The houses are grouped, but separated by a deep recess in the roofline. Michel de Klerk's work here is much more restrained and less exuberant than in the Spaarndammerbuurt **40**. The street walls on Pieter Lodewijk Takstraat are

also by De Klerk. By staggering the housing groups in relation to each other and connecting them with a planter next to the entrances, repeating Z-shaped figurations are created, giving the street walls a dynamic character.

Piet Kramer designed the houses along Burgemeester Tellegenstraat, Willem Passtoorsstraat and Talmastraat. The most impressive is the corner building on Pieter Lodewijk Takstraat, where curving vertical planes rise from the stepped rounded street facades. The two schools fronting the complex on the Amstel Canal side were designed by the Public Works Department. Hildo Krop made the sculptures at the entrances. The Coöperatiehof (1925-1927) is also by Kramer. At Burgemeester Tellegenstraat 128 is a visitor centre, part of the Amsterdam School Museum Het Schip **40**. Architecture critic J.P. Mieras wondered about the project in the architectural weekly *Bouwkundig Weekblad* in 1923: 'Is it Baroque, is it Expressionism, is it a bit of bravado, is it a statement, is it daredevilry, or is it proof of mastery?'

For this complex of 85 houses and one shop, Margaret Staal-Kropholler (1891-1966) only designed the facades. The houses have standard floor plans and were built by four different owner-builders. The aesthetics committee, which included husband Frits Staal (1879-1940), ruled in favour of the facade design. The complex is symmetrical in design with a central section that is set back two metres. The transitions are designed as a kind of sweeping wave. This is all the more beautiful because opposite those waves there is always a side street. There are balconies in the waves. The upper edge of the block, consisting of a long strip of windows and a strip of vertically applied roof tiles, is intersected in a few places by a decorative brick plane with flagpole. Of particular note are the zigzag windows at the entrances.

Holendrechtstraat 1-47
M. Staal-Kropholler
1921-1922

The Staal Family

Margaret Staal-Kropholler was the first woman in the Netherlands to work as a professional architect. Margaret Kropholler worked at the firm of her elder brother Alexander Jacobus, who was associated with Frits Staal. Margaret and Frits, who was married, had a love affair that marked the end of the Staal & Kropholler architectural firm. Frits Staal's son Arthur (1907-1993) was also an architect. In addition to social housing in Theodorus Dobbestraat in Slotermeer (1953) **45**, a rowing club building on Hobbemakade 122 (1954) and the Metropool building on Weesperstraat 99 (1966), the 1971 winner of the Prix de Rome 1935 also built the distinctive A'dam Tower **30**.

71 Housing

Johan M. Coenenstraat, Bartholomeus ⚐
Ruloffsstraat, Bronckhorststraat
J.F. Staal
1922-1924

This U-shaped block contains 108 houses and was designed by architect Frits Staal (1879-1940) for the Amsterdamsche Coöperatieve Woningvereeniging Samenwerking ('Amsterdam Cooperative Housing Association Collaboration'). As with the housing by architect Hendrik Wijdeveld (1885-1987) in Plan West **43**, this block was designed as one unit, with a regular pattern of windows of equal size. The glass projections at the porches form a rhythmic element in the composition. The two wooden doors at each entrance are set at an angle in the facade; the left door is a mock door with letterboxes. On one side, a decorated brick surface forms the transition to the adjacent Huize Lydia; on the other side, a rounded brick surface forms the transition to the buildings on Bartholomeus Ruloffsstraat and Bronckhorststraat. Here, the stairwells are largely closed and feature wavy brick surfaces, making them a less pronounced rhythmic element in the facade.

Huize Lydia ⚐

Located nearby on Roelof Hartplein are two more beautiful Amsterdam School projects. At No 2 is Huize Lydia ('Lydia House') by architect Jan Boterenbrood (1886-1932). The 1927 building originally served as a home for Roman Catholic women and girls. At No 50 is Het Nieuwe Huis ('The New House'), a home for single men and women, built in 1928 by architect Barend van den Nieuwen Amstel (1883-1957). The 188 apartments shared a dining room, a reading room and a 'bicycle room'.

The ground floor now houses a branch of the public library.

Eat, Drink, Sleep

The mercantile and later tourist city of Amsterdam has traditionally always had many hotels and restaurants. And cafés, of course, especially for locals. The Amstel Hotel from 1867 at Professor Tulpplein 1 by architect Cornelis Outshoorn has plenty of allure, as does the 1890 Victoria Hotel opposite Central Station **1**. This design by architect Johann Henkenhaf was built around two existing houses. Architecturally attractive hotels were also built in later periods. The American Hotel **24** from 1902 and the Grand Hotel Centraal at Vijzelstraat 2-20 from 1928 by architect Gerrit Jan Rutgers are well worth checking out. As are the international-standard hotels Hilton (Huig Maaskant, 1962), Okura (Bernard Bijvoet, 1971), Fletcher (Benthem Crouwel, 2013) and nhow (OMA, 2020).

A new trend is the conversion of existing buildings into hotels, such as The Grand in the former City Hall (1992), the Lloyd Hotel in a youth prison (2004), the Conservatorium Hotel in the former Rijkspostspaarbank (2012), the W Hotel in the Government Office building (2015) **12**, the Conscious Hotel in the workshop building of the former Westergasfabriek (2018) **41** and CitizenM in the Amsterdamsche Bank (2019). One of the more modern buildings converted into a hotel is Aldo van Eyck's colourful Moederhuis **82**. It has been home to the Quentin Zoo Hotel since 2018. Smaller hotels have also found their place in repurposed buildings, such as the Windketelhuisje ('Water-company aeration house') on the former GWL site **42** and the 28 characteristic bridge keeper's houses **5**, which have been used as one-room hotels since 2012. Two Brutalist buildings were also converted into hotels: the Volkskrant building (1962) became the Volkshotel and the Leonardo Hotel moved into an anonymous office tower of the AMRO bank (1971).

Restaurants also favour notable existing locations. A 1903 tram depot in Amsterdam-West was converted into food court De Hallen in 2014. A bridge restaurant **36** was established on an old railway bridge. And the REM Island **39** was also turned into a restaurant. On the GWL site **42**, at the Westergasfabriek **41** and on the NDSM site **35**, restored buildings also house cafés and restaurants. The characteristic A'dam Tower **30** on the north side of the IJ contains several bars and restaurants – including one that rotates – in addition to a hotel.

There have always been many traditional pubs in the city, with Café Karpershoek from 1606 on Martelaarsgracht being the oldest pub and De Drie Fleschjes from 1619 on Gravenstraat being the oldest tasting room. In the 1980s, modern white and sleek grand cafés emerged. And finally, since the 1970s, there have been coffee shops, serving not coffee but soft drugs. In 2023, Mike Tyson opened his own coffee shop in Amsterdam.

72 Synagogue

Heinzestraat 1-3
H. Elte Phzn.
1927-1928
W. Bogtman (art)

On the corner of Jacob Obrechtplein and Heinzestraat, architect Harry Elte (1880-1944) designed this monumental synagogue with two upstairs apartments in 1927. The articulated building masses and closed brick surfaces with stained-glass windows and granite thresholds and bands form a Cubist variant of the Amsterdam School, strongly influenced by the American architect Frank Lloyd Wright.

A front portal and vestibule with marble walls lead to the very tall synagogue. The twelve stained-glass windows in the side walls, designed by Willem Bogtman, depict the twelve tribes of Israel. The Torah Ark, the most important object in the synagogue, stands in an elliptical alcove, topped with polished black marble with gold accents, which stands out all the more in the predominantly cubist décor.

Stolpersteine

On the initiative of German artist Gunter Demnig (1947), nearly 100,000 Stolpersteine have already been placed across Europe. These small brass memorials are placed in the pavement in front of the former homes of people who were deported during the Second World War. At Heinzestraat 19, there is such a 'stumbling block' commemorating singing teacher Marianne Schrijver, who lived here at the beginning of the war until she was betrayed, arrested, deported, and murdered in Sobibor. Stolpersteine

for the Frank family 16 can be found at their homes at Merwedeplein 37/2 in Amsterdam-South and in Aachen.

73 Harmoniehof

Harmoniehof and environs
J.C. van Epen
1919-1923
M.J.E. Lippits (ass.)

Architect Jop van Epen (1880-1960) was one of the most prolific architects of the Amsterdam School, with complexes on Amstelveenseweg, Pieter Lastmankade and in the Diamond Quarter. His finest project is the Harmoniehof, an oasis in the bustling city. Van Epen combined the focus on the overall facade composition of the building block and the decorative use of brick of the Amsterdam School with considerably more functionally designed houses. Originally commissioned to architect Lippits, Van Epen is believed to have designed almost everything. The complex was commissioned by Samenwerking ('Cooperation'), the housing co-operative of municipal officials. Buildings consisting of four-storey blocks surround an elongated park, with details characteristic of Van Epen such as buttresses, elongated stairwell lights and small windows. Two double villas form the end of the green square.

Tulpen aus Amsterdam

The song *Tulpen Uit Amsterdam*, made famous by Dutch singer Herman Emmink, is originally a German song. *Tulpen aus Amsterdam* was written in 1953 by Klaus Günter Neumann after a visit to the bulb region. The lyrics were adapted by Ernst Bader in 1956 and the melody is by schlager music composer Ralf Arnie (pseudonym of Dieter Rasch). The Dutch version dates from 1957. British singer Max Bygraves released the song a year later as *Tulips from Amsterdam*.

Tolstraat 154-160
Brinkman & Van der Vlugt
1925-1927; 1928-1929

During the interwar period, Theosophy, a spiritual, philosophical doctrine based on core values from Western and Eastern religions, had a large following in the Netherlands. The Indian guru Krishnamurti (1895-1986) emerged as a new spiritual world leader, who from 1924 led international conferences in Ommen in the province of Overijssel. Many architects and visual artists, especially those with a modern orientation, were inspired by Theosophy. A meeting centre in the shape of a quarter circle was built in Amsterdam's Tolstraat in 1925. It was designed by Rotterdam architects Johannes Brinkman (1902-1949) and Leendert van der Vlugt (1894-1936), who would later build the world-famous Van Nelle Factory in Rotterdam. The auditorium, with 430 seats plus a 250-seat balcony, has a quarter conical roof with the apex above the stage. The building is made of concrete and finished with stucco. The administration building next door is a purely functionalist building, with strip windows in steel frames and white-plastered Cubist facades. From 1943, it has been used as a synagogue, arthouse Cinétol, a mosque, a public library and, since 2024, as arts centre De Appel.

Febo

The well-known fast-food chain Febo takes its name from Ferdinand Bolstraat, where founder Johan de Borst wanted to set up shop. He eventually ended up on Amstelveenseweg, but the name had already been registered. It started as a bakery shop, but after the first automat was opened in 1960, Febo started focusing on eating 'from the wall'. The 'croquette' is a favourite, but fries with mayonnaise are also a Dutch speciality. It inspired filmmaker Quentin Tarantino, who lived in Amsterdam for six months, to create a famous scene in *Pulp Fiction*.

Vincent (John Travolta):
'You know what they put on French fries in Holland instead of ketchup?'
Jules (Samuel L. Jackson): 'What?'
Vincent: 'Mayonnaise.'
Jules: 'Goddamn!'

75 North/South Line

Station Noord, Noorderpark, Central
Station, Rokin, Vijzelgracht, De Pijp,
Europaplein and Zuid (existing railway
station)
Benthem Crouwel
1996-2018
D. Claerbout, G. van der Kaap, M. Laaper,
H. Liemburg, J. Tee (art)

After the dramatic process of building the first metro line through the
Nieuwmarkt neighbourhood ⑦ in the
1970s, construction of a new metro
line between Amsterdam North and
the Zuidas ⑤⑥ did not start until 2002.
The extensive project had three main
underground challenges: an immersed
tunnel under the IJ and Central
Station ❶, a bored tunnel under the

city's historic centre and a number
of deep-bore stations in a densely
built-up urban environment. The metro
line consists of five underground
and two above-ground stations, all
designed by Benthem Crouwel, the
architectural firm of Jan Benthem
(1952) and Mels Crouwel (1952). The
architects designed the different stations not as buildings, but as extensions of the public space. The specific
solutions needed to fit the stations into
the city were decisive for their individual character. Visual art, which was
used differently in each station, also
played an important role in the design
process.

Weather Engine

In the high central metro hall under
Central Station ❶, a LED screen measuring
2.5 by 23.5 metres shows the impressive
digital artwork *Weather Engine* by Belgian
artist David Claerbout (1969). In a classic
Dutch landscape, a figure, unfazed but
dependent on the weather, is busy day and
night doing all kinds of activities to take
care of his surroundings. The artwork is
connected to the internet to retrieve current weather data.

95

Amstel 51
H.J. van Petersom
1681-1683
Hans van Heeswijk architects, Merkx &
Girod (rest. 2005-2009)

The monumental H'Art Museum, the former Hermitage, was built in 1683 by city architect Hans Janszoon van Petersom (†1709) as a retirement home for the elderly. It is a square complex in an austere, Dutch-classical style surrounding a courtyard garden. The more than 100-metre-long straight front facade on the Amstel River is symmetrical, with stately front steps with a mock entrance in the middle, under a large triangular pediment.

During a large-scale conversion into a museum, architect Hans van Heeswijk (1952) promoted the narrow gate under this landing to the building's main entrance. Through the serene, freely accessible courtyard garden with impressive old chestnut trees, redesigned by landscape architect Michael van Gessel (1948), visitors reach the entrance hall, which then gives access to the various exhibition wings. In collaboration with Merkx & Girod Architects, Van Heeswijk transformed the sombre, closed building into a well-organized and spacious whole with a bright and sleek interior.

Amsterdam Museum

Due to the renovation of its main location in the city centre, the Amsterdam Museum, dedicated to the city's past and present, is temporarily located in the H'Art Museum 76. The renovation and expansion of the old museum building with a new entrance and a publicly accessible Stadshal between Kalverstraat and Nieuwezijds Voorburgwal to a design by Neutelings Riedijk is expected to be completed in 2025.

77 Holocaust Names Memorial

Weesperstraat/Nieuwe Herengracht
D. Libeskind
2016-2021

Located in the former Jewish Quarter, the National Holocaust Names Monument was erected to commemorate the more than 102,000 Dutch victims of the Holocaust. It commemorates all Jews deported from the Netherlands during the Second World War who died in concentration camps or en route and whose graves are not known. Architect Daniel Libeskind (1946), the son of Polish Holocaust survivors, designed a monumental labyrinth of long passageways made of bricks, which together form the

Hebrew text 'in memory of' in the floor plan. These letters recur in the same pattern on top of the two-metre-high brick walls in the form of four stainless steel elements, reflecting the surroundings. Inscribed in each of the monument's more than 102,000 bricks is the name, date of birth and age at death of each individual victim. The bricks are placed in alphabetical order of surname so that visitors can finally find their relatives who disappeared during the war to commemorate them.

Royal Theatre Carré

In a beautiful spot along the Amstel River is the classicist-style Royal Theatre Carré. The building was an initiative of the travelling circus family Carré, who created a permanent home for their horse shows here in 1887. The building, designed by J.P.F. van Rossem and W.J. Vuyk, has a horseshoe-shaped auditorium with 1756 seats. Carré is used for a variety of shows and has become the most famous theatre of the Netherlands.

78 Weesperflat

Weesperstraat 7-57
H. Hertzberger
1959-1966
T. Hazewinkel, H.A. Dicke (ass.)

In the early 1960s, Herman Hertzberger (1932) built this student flat building when he was starting out as an architect. At that time, Weesperstraat was being widened to make the city centre more accessible to car traffic and, with new buildings, took on a modern and large-scale character. In the seven-storey building, Hertzberger's later design philosophy of 'creating space, leaving space' was already present. A characteristic feature of the building is its openness. 'Entering' the building proceeds gradually along covered outdoor spaces, through level differences and lighting effects, and Hertzberger also designed the concrete seating elements. The student rooms face a double corridor, with stairs and lifts and sanitary facilities in the middle zone, and have a communal sitting and dining area with a terrace. On the fourth floor, there is an interior street with a balcony that was freely accessible at the time. Through its horizontal articulation with an upper and a lower level, the design connects to the canal houses around the corner.

The locomotive

As a reminder of the demolished railway station on this site, at one of the entrances to Weesperplein metro station stands the sculpture *De ontwikkeling van de locomotief* ('The development of the locomotive'), designed by architect Piet Kramer. It shows three different locomotives that once departed from this spot: a steam locomotive, an electric locomotive and a diesel locomotive. Installed in 1941, the sculpture was originally part of a bridge also designed by Kramer.

Vrolikstraat 8
De Geus & Ingwersen
1952-1956
H.M.M. op de Laak, W. Reijers (art)

As is usual for a vocational school, the workshops and theory and practice rooms were housed in different parts of the building. Forging, welding and car workshops were combined on the ground floor with the teachers' room and entrance hall. On the four floors were theory and practical classrooms for benchwork and woodwork. On the fourth floor were the canteen and gymnasium. The building, a design by architects Commer de Geus (1889-1957) and Ben Ingwersen (1921-1996),

has a concrete skeleton structure, which is left visible in the interior. The facades are defined by a lattice-work of vibrated concrete elements with deep, angled reveals/jambs. The emergency stairwell is clad with decorative elements of vibrated concrete. Partly because of the concrete rooftop structure for the ventilators, the building looks like an homage to French architect Le Corbusier's Unités d'Habitation. Since 2013, the school Cygnus Gymnasium has been the user and the building has been renovated. The building is an example of Brutalism, which is experiencing a reappraisal in the early twenty-first century.

Wibaut

In the middle of Wibautstraat is a monument commemorating city councillor Floor Wibaut (1859-1936), nicknamed 'the Mighty' or 'the Viceroy of Amsterdam'. The 1967 sculpture by artist Han Wezelaar (1901-1984) originally stood somewhere else, but Wibautstraat is obviously a more suitable location. Wibaut, as a Social Democrat councillor from 1914 to 1931, accomplished a great deal in the field of public housing. Who builds? Wibaut builds!

Plantage Middenlaan 2a
J.M. van der Meij; ZJA
1910-1915; 1990-1993

The Hortus Botanicus is one of the oldest botanical gardens in the world. The Hortus was established in 1638 by the Amsterdam city council to cultivate medicinal herbs and plants. The current location has been in use since 1682. The Orangery was built in 1870. In 1915, an existing laboratory was extended and fitted with a new facade by architect Joan Melchior van der Meij (1878-1949). It is an early example of Amsterdam School architecture. The Hortus of the University of Amsterdam has been an independent organization since 1986. The dilapidated greenhouses have been replaced by a modern triangular greenhouse, a design by ZJA, the architectural firm of Moshé Zwarts (1937-2019) and Rein Jansma (1959-2023), with a clear height ranging from four to eleven metres. Three zones have been created with subtropical, tropical and desert climates. High up in the greenhouse is a footbridge with a glass floor. The greenhouse is constructed from standard elements used in greenhouse construction. The main load-bearing structure, based on the tensegrity principle, is on the outside.

'So they canal see us'

On Saturday 6 June 1964, The Beatles enjoyed a boat tour through Amsterdam before performing in Blokker, North Holland, in the evening. Beatlemania was at its peak and the canal cruise attracted massive interest. Several fans jumped into the water to reach the boat, but were nabbed by police. Near the final destination, the Doelen Hotel, there was a near collision with flat-bottomed boat De Tijdgeest ('The Zeitgeist'). Among the youngsters on its deck were future 'starchitect' Rem Koolhaas and his younger

brother Thomas, who even managed to jump into the Beatle boat. George Harrison commented: 'This is absolutely wonderful – crazy chaos.' And a word-playing John Lennon: 'So they canal see us.'

81 Artis 🏛 ☕ 🍴

Plantage Kerklaan 38
G.B. Salm, A. Salm
1838; 1866-1868; 1879-1882

Artis, founded in 1838 by the zoological society Natura Artis Magistra, is the oldest zoo in the Netherlands. The landscaped park has 27 monumental buildings, mostly from the nineteenth century. Gerlof Salm (1831-1897) was the zoo's resident architect for 35 years. After designing the Library Building (1866-1868, Plantage Middenlaan 45), he and his son Abraham Salm (1857-1915) realized the imposing Aquarium Building (1879-1882, Plantage Middenlaan 53), which at the time was the largest and most modern in the world. It was built in a neo-classical style with classic columns and a dome. At the corner of Plantage Kerklaan and Plantage Middenlaan is the freely accessible Artis Square, which is enclosed by two monumental buildings, the 1868 Founder's Room by G.B. Salm and the oldest building of Artis from 1855, which now houses the Groote Museum.

Oldest Tree

Artis is not only a zoo, but with more than 700 trees, it is also an official arboretum. The garden is home to Amsterdam's oldest tree, the so-called Heijman oak. It was planted in the late eighteenth century, making it much older than the zoo itself. Artis also has an Anne Frank tree. This was grown from the horse chestnut that Anne Frank saw from the Secret Annexe 16 during the war years.

Public Green and Parks

Already during the construction of the ring of canals in the seventeenth century, trees were planted along the canals. With those trees, Amsterdam has traditionally been a relatively green city. With the densification of the old city and the large increase in the population in densely built working-class neighbourhoods, public green spaces in the form of city parks and public gardens became necessary at the end of the nineteenth century. Relatively late compared to other Dutch cities and initially on private initiative. The centrally located Vondelpark 59, created in 1865 by a group of wealthy and prominent Amsterdammers, grew to become Amsterdam's most popular city park. At the entrance to the park is a 2.3-metre-high bronze statue of its namesake, the seventeenth-century poet Joost van den Vondel, holding a book and a quill. Sarphatipark (1885) was also the result of a private initiative, this time by the doctor and benefactor Samuel Sarphati (1813-1866), who played an important role in the development of education and public health in Amsterdam; the Sarphati monument can be found in the park. The Westerpark near the Westergasfabriek 41, opened in 1891, was also the only bit of green space in a densely built-up nineteenth-century neighbourhood at the time.

The 12-hectare Oosterpark from 1891 is the first park made by the municipality, with an iron bandstand from 1908. It was designed by landscape architect Leonard Anthony Springer (1855-1940). Oosterpark is home to a number of memorials: the National Monument to the History of Slavery 91 where the abolition of slavery is commemorated each year, and Jeroen Henneman's sculpture De Schreeuw ('The Scream') commemorating the terrorist murder of Dutch filmmaker and columnist Theo van Gogh in 2004. These first landscaped Amsterdam city parks are characterized by a romantic layout with winding paths and sinuous water features in an English garden style. They have fences all around and gates that can be closed at night.

In 1928, it was decided to build the nearly 1,000-hectare Amsterdamse Bos ('Amsterdam Forest'), a design by urban planners Cornelis van Eesteren (1897-1988) and Jakoba Mulder (1900-1988), who later incorporated it into the city's General Expansion Plan (AUP). The forest, which is roughly five times as large as any other park and parkland in Amsterdam, was built as an unemployment relief work project during the Great Depression of the 1930s. The Bosbaan, a rowing course, and sports fields are part of the park. The Beatrixpark in Amsterdam South from 1938 was also an unemployment relief project. This park was part of the international horticultural exhibition Floriade in 1972. It was held in the nearby, newly developed 45-hectare Amstelpark. Several pavilions, the Glass House and the Rhododendron Valley are reminders of this event. A green strip connects the Amstelpark and the Amsterdamse Bos.

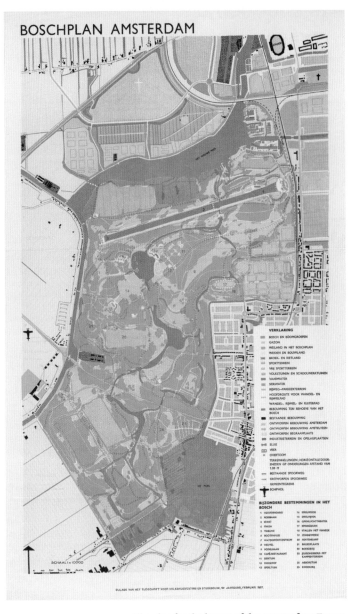

The plan for the layout of the Amsterdam Forest.

Cemeteries are also often green oases in the city. The tree-lined De Nieuwe Ooster, designed by landscape architect Leonard Anthony Springer in 1892, houses the special Funeral Museum. Many local celebrities are buried at Zorgvlied cemetery 68 along the Amstel River.

82 Moederhuis

Plantage Middenlaan 33
A.E. van Eyck
1973-1978

The colourful Moederhuis (Mother House) was designed by architect Aldo van Eyck (1918-1999) as a temporary shelter for 16 parents and about 78 children. It was built in a gap in a nineteenth-century street wall in combination with the restoration of two adjacent historical buildings. The infill adapted to the existing structure (building height, vertical main layout, substructure), but also deviated radically from it. The position of the entrance and stairwell is such that it effectively created two buildings: a high-rise and a lower extension of the existing buildings. Even during construction, in addition to colour-coding the low-rise buildings with purple, red, orange, yellow and green, Van Eyck decided to paint the metal facades of the high-rise buildings in different colours as well, thus enhancing the articulation of the facade. 'I don't pick colours; my favourite colour is the rainbow.' The building still houses a childcare centre. The upper floors are used as a hotel.

Holocaust Museum

Plantage Middenlaan 24, 27 and 29 is home to the National Holocaust Museum. The complex consists of two buildings: the theatre Hollandsche Schouwburg – the assembly point from which Jews were deported to concentration camps during the Second World War – and the teacher training centre Hervormde Kweekschool, from which Jewish children were taken to hiding addresses. Both buildings have been brought together in a succession of spaces by Office Winhov in 2024 to create an impressive memorial site.

Henri Polaklaan 9
H.P. Berlage
1898-1900
L. Zijl, J. Eisenloeffel, R.N. Roland Holst
(art)

The Algemeene Nederlandsche Diamantbewerkersbond ('General Diamond Workers' Union of the Netherlands', ANDB), one of the first trade unions in the Netherlands, commissioned architect Hendrik Petrus Berlage (1856-1934) to design their headquarters. Berlage worked for the corporate sector and was employed by the Kröller-Müller firm, but he was also a socialist and designed buildings for workers' cooperative Voorwaarts ('Forwards'), a monument to socialist Spiekman, and a mausoleum for Lenin. The building contained meeting rooms, office space, a library with reading room and an archive. The main entrance is marked by a massive entrance arch with wide front steps and a tower. The windows, grouped three-by-three, form a regular pattern in the facade, which is finished with a border of battlements. The centrepiece of the building is the central stairwell, with daylight from a glass roof, with patterns of yellow and white glazed brick and natural stone columns and balustrades. With its tall tower, cast-iron wall anchors and battlement-like roof ornaments, the building resembles a medieval castle (burcht in Dutch). For a while, 'De Burcht van Berlage' housed the National Trade Union Museum; it is still used by the trade union FNV.

Diamond Industry

The diamond industry was an important pillar of Amsterdam's economy. Two diamond-cutting factories recall that era: the Boas Brothers building on Nieuwe Uilenburgerstraat 173-175 by architect J.W. Meijer from 1879 (still in use by Gassan) and the Asscher building on Tolstraat 127-129 by architect G. van Arkel from 1907. The 1910 Diamond Exchange at Weesperplein 4b, also designed by Gerrit

van Arkel, was converted into the Capital C creative hub by architecture firm ZJA in 2018.

Entrepotdok 59-78, 87-98
J. de Greef/A.J. & J. van Stigt
1827-1829/1982-1988

The former 1827 Algemeen Rijks-Entrepot was a duty-free government warehouse for transit goods. As such, the complex was behind high walls for a long time. The characteristic warehouses were designed by city architect Jan de Greef (1784-1834). They are five or six metres wide and thirty metres deep. The badly neglected complex with a total length of five hundred metres was renovated in the mid-1980s by architects Joop van Stigt (1934-2011) and his son André (1959) into social housing and business premises. The lower floors have been utilized for parking spaces, storage areas and business units. To provide the dwellings with sufficient daylight, the heart of the building block has been hollowed out. The facades and wooden floor and roof structures have been left intact as much as possible. Under the monumental roof are now artist residences and communal homes.

Amsterdammertje

To protect the pavement from (illegally) parked cars, all over Amsterdam there are bollards about 75 centimetres in height: Amsterdammertjes. Originally these bollards were made of cast iron, but since the 1970s they have been made of sheet steel. The three crosses refer to the city's coat of arms. Other solutions for keeping cars out are increasingly being adopted and the number of bollards in the city centre is decreasing. But you can still buy this symbol of Amsterdam in all kinds of versions as a souvenir.

85 Vierwindenhuis

Windroosplein
G.P. Frassinelli
1983-1990

The Vierwindenhuis ('House of Four Winds') was built on the initiative of Dutch philosopher Fons Elders. It was designed in 1983 by Italian architect Gian Piero Frassinelli (1939). The collective residential building with communal facilities (café, crèche, studios and a workshop) is based on a cosmological order and oriented towards the Pole Star. Each of the four corners, where most of the communal facilities are housed, is dedicated to one of the elements. The complex was to create conditions for a way of living that could break the traditional relationship between seclusion and interaction with fellow occupants. References to the Amsterdam School and structuralist and organic architecture are apparent in the architectural design.

Superstudio

Architect Gian Piero Frassinelli, together with Adolfo Natalini (1941-2020) and several other architects, founded the avant-garde collective Superstudio in 1966. Their most radical idea was the Continuous Monument: An Architectural Model for Total Urbanization, a brutally abstract grid applicable anywhere in the world. Superstudio inspired famous architects such as Rem Koolhaas and Zaha Hadid. The members themselves didn't really build anything revolutionary: mainly picturesque brick buildings and retro architecture.

Piet Heinkade/Oostelijke Handelskade
Various architects
1996-2007

The area along the IJhaven harbour forms the link between the city centre and the new residential areas in the Eastern Docklands. A few remaining warehouses form the basis and inspiration for a series of robust buildings along Piet Heinkade and the Eastern Quay. The typology of warehouses was also used in the architectural elaboration: solid brick buildings with small window openings. Near that centre are cultural buildings such as 3xN's Muziekgebouw ('Music Building', 2005) and the Passenger Terminal for cruise ships. There are also office buildings and residential complexes and the restored De Zwijger warehouse as a cultural enclave. In Rietlandpark, individual buildings have been placed in a green zone: five residential towers by VenhoevenCS (2001) and five office towers by Hans van Heeswijk (2001). The elegant IJ Tower by Neutelings Riedijk (1998) marks the transition to the islands of the Eastern Docklands.

Pakhuis De Zwijger ⬙ ☕ 🍴 ⊕

At Piet Heinkade 179 stood a refrigerated warehouse for perishables, built in 1934 by architect Jan de Bie Leuveling Tjeenk (1885-1940) for the Blaauwhoedenveem ('Blue hats warehousing company'). The robust warehouse has a structure of concrete mushroom columns and a block-built brick facade to emphasize its non-load-bearing character. Initially, De Zwijger ('The Silent') was supposed to be demolished. A road was built right through it and the building was given a cultural function after a restoration by architect André van Stigt.

Javakade/Sumatrakade and environs
Soeters Van Eldonk Ponec
1991-2000

In response to the large scale and formal urbanism of the previously developed, adjacent KNSM Island **88**, architect Sjoerd Soeters (1947) designed a small-scale, variegated, high-density urban structure for Java Island. On Sumatrakade on the northern IJ side, the buildings stand seven layers high, and on the southern Javakade five layers. Four newly dug cross canals with contemporary canal houses provide a subdivision of the homogeneous building mass. Green zones lie between the building blocks, linked by a cycle route along the entire length of the island. The reason for having more than one architect work on a single block is to try to attain the variety found in central Amsterdam's canal frontages. On the east side of the island is an anomalous building: live-work building Wladiwostok by Belgian architect Jo Crépain from 1995.

Hotel Jakarta ☕ 🍴 🛏

On the western tip of Java Island, Hotel Jakarta, designed by architectural firm SeARCH, was completed in 2018. The hotel rooms were completely prefabricated as modules and assembled on site in a mostly wooden support structure. At the heart of the building is a subtropical indoor garden realized in collaboration with the Hortus Botanicus **80**. The open wall with objects and suitcases refers to the ocean liners that departed from here to the former colony of the Dutch East Indies.

KNSM-laan/Levantkade
H.F. Kollhoff, Chr. Rapp
1989-1994

The harbours of the Eastern Docklands were built at the end of the nineteenth century to replace the old harbours, which were too small and had moreover become inaccessible due to the construction of a railway line. In the 1960s, with the advent of container transport and ever-larger ships, these docklands fell into disuse as well. As the port functions fell away, the area was transformed from a largely inaccessible dockland and industrial area into a lively residential area from the 1980s onwards.

The first housing development arose on the Entrepot site based on a masterplan by Atelier Pro. The former cattle market and abattoir site has been turned into a business park and a residential area with about six hundred social housing units. The urban plan for KNSM Island envisaged developing a closed harbour front, analogous to the former quay buildings. Architect Jo Coenen (1949) designed a plan with large robust housing blocks that match the scale of the harbours. Some of the buildings that were to be preserved were included in the structure of these large blocks. Coenen himself was responsible for the round residential building at the head of the pier. Two large closed building blocks

were assigned to foreign architects: the Belgian Bruno Albert (1941-2023) scrupulously followed the main urban design form: a rectangular six-storey building block with a round eight-storey section in the centre. German architect Hans Kollhoff (1946) took a more liberal approach to the principles. To spare an existing building, the building block was folded around it. The Piraeus residential building is inspired by the heavy, industrial character of warehouses and port buildings. The sculptural block gradually rises up from the south side; on the KNSM-laan it is a brutally heavy block, while angular oblique lines dominate the inner courtyards. The steel windows with their graphic subdivisions underline the industrial character of the building. Private properties and rental units have been realized in a wide range of floor plans. Visual artist Arno van der Mark (1949) designed the colonnade in the gateway in the west facade.

The striking building was a radical departure from mainstream building practice and set the tone for architecture in the following years. It marked the return of the closed building block, and dark brick became ubiquitous afterwards.

C. van Eesterenlaan and environs
West 8
1994-1999

For the two piers Borneo and Sporenburg, urban design office West 8 developed a low-rise plan with a density of a hundred houses per hectare: long building strips divided into narrow three-storey plots. The sea of low-rises is interrupted by three large residential buildings that relate to the large scale of the docklands: The Whale by architect Frits van Dongen (1946), Pacman by Koen van Velsen (1952) and Hoop Liefde Fortuin ('Hope Love Fortune') by Rudy Uytenhaak

(1949). Building De Oceaan from 1951 on R.J.H. Fortuynplein is the only remnant of the maritime past. Along Scheepstimmermanstraat, a varied series of contiguous houses by different architects have been built. These are the first free plots the municipality of Amsterdam has offered to individuals to build on themselves in a long time.

The Whale

One of the three large-scale objects that interrupt the low-rise buildings of Borneo and Sporenburg is residential building The Whale (Baron G.A. Tindalplein), built by architect Frits van Dongen (de Architekten Cie.) between 1995 and 2000. The rectangular volume has been warped so that all dwellings receive sufficient daylight. Elevating the corners created entrance areas. The facades are clad in zinc, with wood-clad galleries lining the courtyard. The city garden in the courtyard was designed by West 8.

90 Funenpark

Funenpark
F.J. van Dongen (de Architekten Cie.)
i.c.w. various architects
1998-2008

Funen was an old industrial estate
on the Eastern Islands in the bend of
the Amsterdam-Utrecht railway line.
A large L-shaped apartment building
with 305 dwellings by urban designer
Frits van Dongen (1946) acts as a visual
and acoustic barrier for the area.
A railway transformer station has been
incorporated into that peripheral construction. To this end, a 35-metre
steel overpass has been installed,
completely hidden behind the brick
facade. Above it there is student housing. In the car-free, park-like inner area
are sixteen small individual blocks

with up to twelve homes, the Hidden
Delights, a reference to different
kinds of chocolates in one box. They
were designed by NL Architects, DKV
Architects, Erna van Sambeek, Geurst
& Schulze, Kuiper Compagnons and
Dick van Gameren.

Between Time

During archaeological research prior to
the construction of the neighbourhood – in
addition to all kinds of shards of plates
and jugs – they came across the still almost
intact 26th stronghold of the defensive
wall around the city from 1663. Artist
Gabriel Lester (1972) was commissioned
to create a sculpture in which the history
of the site would be (partly) visible and
tangible. *Tussentijd* (Between Time) consists of five huge shards with an exterior of
Corten steel and an interior of smoothly
polished steel, symbolizing past and
present. On the outside are maps of the
surrounding area.

Linnaeusstraat 2
J.J. van Nieukerken, M.A. van Nieukerken
1911-1926
J. Bronner, W.O.J. Nieuwenkamp, W.M.M.
Retera, J.L. Vreugde (art)

After a complicated run-up, during which architect Johan van Nieukerken (1854-1913) died and the First World War caused material shortages, it was under the direction of his son Marie van Nieukerken (1879-1963) that the new Royal Tropical Institute was completed in 1926, after ten years of construction. The design is traditional and historicizing in a Renaissance Revival style. Also in terms of materials, applied art and symbolism, the building reflects the views held on the Dutch colonies at the time. The huge building, the city's largest at the time, consists of two interconnected parts: the ethnological museum with a three-storey light hall with monumental staircases and surrounding galleries, and the institute building with library and auditorium. The building was lavishly decorated for its day and adorned with numerous symbolic sculptures and ornaments. A special Symbolism Commission oversaw its realization.

Monument to the History of Slavery

The National Monument to the History of Slavery, a design by Surinamese sculptor Erwin de Vries (1926-2018), was unveiled by Queen Beatrix in 2002, 139 years after the abolition of slavery in the Dutch colonies on 1 July 1863. Every year, a commemoration of these 'broken chains', Keti Koti, takes place at the monument in Oosterpark. The bronze sculpture group consists of three parts: the shackled

slavery past, the breaking of the contemporary wall of discrimination and the flight to a better future.

92 Housing Rochdale

1e Atjehstraat, Molukkenstraat
J.E. van der Pek
1909-1911

Architect Jan van der Pek (1865-1919) was one of the pioneers of social housing in Amsterdam; in 1909, he realized the first housing under the Housing Act in Van Beuningenstraat. In Amsterdam-North, the Van der Pekbuurt was named after him. This project for the Coöperatieve Bouwvereniging Rochdale (cooperative building society) was the first to feature communal gardens: 'oases accessible to all, amid the big-city bustle'. The building blocks end with a 'head block', eliminating the need for complicated corner solutions. The courtyard garden is enclosed by two modest garden houses. Some architectural historians see this project as a first step towards the row housing of the functionalist New Building movement. The ground-floor residents had their own private two-metre garden. The communal garden was originally semi-public and was also used for concerts by a workers' orchestra.

Housing Act

On 22 June 1901, Queen Wilhelmina signed the Housing Act. The government became heavily involved in housing construction. There were now quality requirements for housing and urban planning, and housing corporations gained access to financing for social housing. Specifically, back-to-back houses, bedsteads and alcoves (small rooms without windows) were banned and from then on, every house had to be connected to the (drinking) water supply and have a water closet. The Housing Act also made it possible to

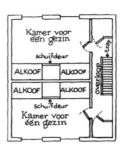

declare substandard houses 'uninhabitable' and force homeowners to improve homes.

Bridges

A city with lots of canals and waterways is also a city with lots of bridges. Over the Amstel, for example, the river from which the city takes its name. One of the most famous bridges over the Amstel River is the Magere Brug ('Skinny Bridge'), which has had its current appearance since as far back as 1691. The bridge has been replaced and repaired several times since then, though. The Blauwbrug ('Blue Bridge') and Hogesluis ('High Lock'), located on either side of the Skinny Bridge, were both installed in 1883 and were modelled after the Parisian bridges over the Seine. A later bridge over the Amstel was designed by architect H.P. Berlage in 1932, as the final part of his urban development plan for Amsterdam-South 63. This bridge was later named the Berlagebrug ('Berlage Bridge').

One of the most prominent designers of bridges in Amsterdam was architect Pieter Lodewijk Kramer (1881-1961). From 1913 until his retirement in 1952, he designed around 500 bridges in the service of the Public Works Department, of which some 220 were built. All his bridges are designed in Amsterdam School style and usually with sculptures by city sculptor Hildo Krop (1884-1970). His bridges are often equipped with benches, lanterns and kiosks. He also designed the bridge keeper's houses. Of particular note are the 1915 bridge over the Waalseilandsgracht near the Shipping House 3 and the 1928 Lyceum Bridge by Olympiaplein 58. Kramer also designed 78 mostly wooden bridges in the Amsterdam Forest. Architects Dick Slebos (1923-2001) and Dirk Sterenberg (1921-1996) were appointed as Kramer's successors. Slebos designed the bridges over the Slotervaart (1956-1960) and Sterenberg the graceful viaduct in the Cornelis Lelylaan (1962).

Bridges have an important symbolic value as access points to new neighbourhoods. Ton Venhoeven's Jan Schaefer Bridge from 2001 leads to Java Island 87. The nine small bridges on Java Island itself were designed by Belgian artist couple Rombouts-Droste. At Borneo-Sporenburg 89, West 8 designed three bright-red steel bridges, including the spectacular Python Bridge. The Enneüs Heerma Bridge to IJburg 98, designed by British architect Nicholas Grimshaw, was emphatically designed as a 'landmark'. Nearby here is the Nescio Bridge by the also British WilkinsonEyre architects, a bicycle bridge over the Amsterdam-Rhine Canal.

And then there is the Staalmeesters bridge over Groenburgwal, where Claude Monet made his painting of the Zuiderkerk church around 1874. This 'love lock bridge' is constantly being stripped of padlocks, as the structure cannot support all that metal. Fortunately for new sweethearts, new love bridges are constantly being found in Amsterdam.

Julianaplein 1
H.G.J. Schelling
1937-1939
P. Alma, Th. van Reijn (art);
Office Winhov (ren. 2016-2021)

Amstel Station is the most important building in the oeuvre of railway architect Herman Schelling (1888-1978), who built almost twenty different station buildings for the Dutch Railways from 1913 until his retirement in 1954. Completed in 1939 on the then outskirts of Amsterdam, Amstel Station was the first transport hub in the Netherlands where different modes of transport (train, tram, bus, bicycle, pedestrian, car and later metro) could all come. Schelling collaborated on his design with urban planner Cornelis van Eesteren and city architect Jan Leupen. The central station hall with large canopies on either side is the link between train and city traffic and, with its large glass surfaces and exposed steel portal frames, is an example of functionalist architecture. The closed end walls feature enormous murals by artist Peter Alma (1886-1969) on the theme of rail transport. A striking feature of the building is that, as one of the few station buildings in the Netherlands, it stands at right angles to the direction of the tracks.

Witkar

Amsterdam Provo city councillor Luud Schimmelpennink (1935) developed a collective inner-city car-sharing system in the early 1970s. Participants in the project could rent a white cart, an electrically powered vehicle for two people, with a top speed of 30 kilometres per hour, at one of the five charging stations. During the 1980s, the project was discontinued as the necessary scale-up proved unfeasible. A total of 38 white carts were built; the Amsterdam

Museum **76**, Nemo **4** and the Design Museum in Den Bosch all have one in their collection.

Brink, Onderlangs and environs
Various architects
1921-1928

Due to the great housing shortage and high material and construction prices after the First World War, architects and municipalities sought alternatives to traditional construction. Concrete was cheap and unskilled workers could work with it. In part of Watergraafsmeer, a garden village was built with experimental concrete houses in eight different building systems, such as Isotherme, Winget and Olbertz: Betondorp, which translates as Concrete Village. The urban plan and the buildings around the central square, the Brink, are by architect Dick Greiner (1891-1964). Around the Brink are a few larger houses, shops, a library and a community centre. In Graanstraat and Schoovenstraat, architect Han van Loghem (1881-1940) designed functional business-like facades with abstract decorations above the entrances of the houses. Betondorp was also known for its residents, predominantly communists and socialists, who therefore would not sanction a café in their 'village'. There is one now.

Number 14

Betondorp's most famous son is undoubtedly Johan Cruijff. The best footballer the Netherlands has ever known grew up at Akkerstraat 32. Father Cruijff had a shop there selling vegetables, fruit and potatoes. Cruijff was born on 25 April 1947 in the Burgerziekenhuis hospital on Linnaeusstraat. It was only natural for Johan to join Ajax, the Watergraafsmeer club. He later rose to even greater fame with Barcelona, Ajax again and archrival Feyenoord. He was also successful as the coach of Ajax and Barcelona. Johan Cruijff played 48 matches as an international. He died on 24 March 2016.

Groesbeekdreef and environs
G.S. Nassuth
(Urban Development Department)
1962-1973

In the early 1960s, planning began for a large-scale expansion district to the east of the city. Inspired by the CIAM ideas of the 1930s of high-rise buildings set in a green environment, this 'city for the year 2000' was built. Identical high-rise blocks with concrete facades in a honeycomb pattern, placed in a park landscape. The street level is for pedestrians and cyclists; car traffic and the metro pass through the neighbourhood on viaducts.

A circuit of raised streets connects the high-rises with each other and with the car parks. Already during construction, criticism and negative publicity prevailed and from the outset the neighbourhood was plagued by vacancy and vandalism. Many optimistic proposals and refurbishments notwithstanding, it was finally decided to densify the neighbourhood with low-rise buildings and demolish almost all the 'problem flats'.

Anton de Kom

In 1934, Surinamese writer Anton de Kom (1898-1945) published his book *Wij slaven van Suriname (We slaves of Surinam)*. A communist, he was active in the Dutch resistance during the Second World War. He was arrested and died in a German concentration camp. Around 2000, the Anton de Komplein square was built in the Bijlmermeer 95, home to many Surinamese and Antillean Dutch from the former colonies. A bronze statue by artist Jikke van Loon (1971) was placed here in 2006. The statue is not without controversy.

The stripped body would portray De Kom as enslaved and as a 'savage native', and the severed hand would be a reference to corporal punishment.

Dostojevskisingel, Dolingadreef and
environs
C.J.M. Weeber
1980-1982

In response to the small-scale mania
and 'cauliflower' neighbourhoods of
the 1970s, architect Carel Weeber
(1937) returned to the classic closed
building block in designing this neighbourhood. The neighbourhood contains 3800 portico houses in sixteen
four- and five-storey blocks. The robust
building blocks have publicly accessible green courtyards, reached via
gates, and were designed by different architects. The blocks have
canted corners and face 30-metre-
wide streets. There are two anomalous building blocks: a rounded block
near the bend in the metro line and an
80 by 240-metre superblock between
Dantestraat and Daniël Defoestraat
by Carel Weeber himself. The original
brick stringcourses have disappeared
under a layer of plaster, but the large 1
on the facade has been retained.

Bijlmerbajes

The Over-Amstel Penitentiary Centre,
better known as the Bijlmerbajes, was
completed in 1978. Designed by architect
couple Joop Pot (1909-1973) and Koosje
Pot-Keegstra (1908-1997), the complex
with tower buildings was very modern for
its time. Not only in terms of architecture,
but also because of its humane design,
where inmates were housed in small
social groups. There were also initially no
bars on the windows. Since July 2017, the
complex is no longer used as a prison. One
of the towers remains as a 'green tower'
with a park and urban agriculture;

the rest is being demolished and will be
replaced by a car-free residential area
with 1,350 homes in residential towers.

Bijlmerplein 888
Alberts & Van Huut
1979-1987

To everyone's surprise, in 1979, the Nederlandsche Middenstandsbank (NMB) chose the organic architecture of Ton Alberts (1927-1999) for its headquarters, giving the traditional bank image of reliability and tradition a completely new expression. The sloping forms in the interior and exterior would allow people to be freer and more creative in their work here. But the sloping lines also improve daylighting, traffic noise reduction and indoor acoustics. Furthermore, the forms are structurally logical and the heavy massive inner cavity wall plays an important role in energy management, as an accumulator. The windows are relatively small. The building, with 34,000 square metres of office space for 2,500 employees at the time, consists of ten tower-like clusters of varying heights connected on the ground floor by an interior street. After the bank's departure, the building was renovated into 263 homes, offices, hospitality and a school under the name Zandkasteel (Sandcastle) in 2020.

Rudolf Steiner

The architecture of Ton Alberts and Max van Huut (1947) gave impetus to anthroposophical or organic building in the Netherlands. This movement is based on the work of Rudolf Steiner (1861-1925) and his monumental 1920 Goetheanum in Dornach, Switzerland. In the 1920s, the architects Buijs and Lürsen introduced this architectural style to the Netherlands with the Rudolf Steiner Clinic in The Hague. Later, organic forms were mainly applied to churches and Waldorf schools. SeARCH's 2014 Geert Groote College (Frederik Roeskestraat 84) is a contemporary interpretation of organic building.

IJburglaan and environs
Palmboom & Van den Bout, H+N+S
1995-2010

IJburg consists of seven artificial islands, which together will form a residential district for 40,000 residents. The 2001 Enneüs Heermabrug by British architect Nicholas Grimshaw (1939) provides access to the central IJburglaan, the main access where the tram also runs. Each island has its own character. The Haveneiland (Marina Island) section, built first, is based on a rectangular grid of large city blocks. On the Rieteilanden (Reed islands, around Lisdoddelaan), private residential houses by various architects have been built. The more informal Steigereiland (Jetty Island, around Jan Olphert Vaillantlaan and Cornelis Zillesenlaan) also largely consists of a collage of contiguous and detached private residences. Floating houses and the striking Sluishuis 99 have also been realized here. Centrumeiland (Centre Island), Middeneiland (Middle Island) and Strandeiland (Beach Island) are under development. Buiteneiland (Outer Island) will be a nature island with facilities for sports, recreation and culture.

Pampus Plan

In 1965, architectural firm Van den Broek & Bakema developed a study plan for a residential area in the IJsselmeer lake for 350,000 people. A ribbon city ten kilometres long on four artificial islands. With wide motorways, a monorail and high-rise buildings, it was a typical example of 1960s urban planning. The tall buildings, mostly offices, along the 14-lane motorway were to form a soundproof wall. Thirty years later, the development of the IJburg district began.

Haringbuisdijk 905
BIG, Barcode Architects
2016-2022

The rather uniform IJburg district 98 gained a spectacular residential build-ing, the Sluishuis ('Lock House') by Danish architect Bjarke Ingels (1974), as an urban landmark in 2022. The 442 apartments are grouped in one square, closed building block, with triangular sections taken from this volume on two sides. The result is a sculptural main form and massive overhangs. The tri-angular incision at the bottom offers views over the water from the court-yard. The tip extends a whopping 52 metres. The incision at the opposite top leads to a stepped structure. Here there is a publicly accessible walking route up to the roof, the 'stairways to heaven'. The jetty for houseboats is also public.

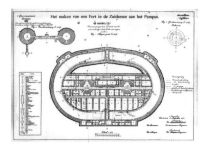

Fort Island Pampus

Pampus was the name of a shipping chan-nel in the former Zuiderzee, which kept silting up. Often heavily laden ships could not pass through it, and this is what the expression 'voor Pampus liggen' ('lying at Pampus') recalls. To bypass Pampus, first the North Holland Canal (1824) and later the North Sea Canal (1876) were dug. In 1887, the artificial island of Pampus was built in the IJmeer with a fort, which was part of the Defence Line of Amsterdam. The island can be reached by ferry from IJburg.

Krijn Taconiskade 1-567
Orange Architects
2017-2022

Orange Architects is the office of Jeroen Schipper (1966) and Patrick Meijers (1971). Their sculptural contemporary residential building on IJburg 98 is completely energy-neutral and includes a host of communal facilities, such as a living room, a cinema, a yoga studio, lounge and work space, guest rooms and a rooftop landscape with a bar. By placing the nearly three hundred apartments in the outer envelope, an impressively tall, wood-framed meandering 'canyon' has been created inside the building, with a ramp connecting all the shared spaces. The glass roof over this interior space acts as a water feature on the communal roof garden, which is laid out as an undulating dune landscape with pines. As a contrast to the wooden interior, the facades of this collective residential building are clad in dark, pre-patinated zinc. The wooden rock at the front, which also gives access to the car park, serves as a play area and as a stand during events.

De Warren

Amsterdam has been experimenting with new forms of housing for over a century. A new offshoot of this housing rooted in experimentation is the self-build housing cooperative De Warren, which has built a 'nature-inclusive, energy-positive, collective' and almost entirely wooden residential building on Nydia Ecurystraat with 36 sustainable apartments with many communal spaces for its own members (Natrufied Architecture, 2023).

Index of names

Credits

This book is published in collaboration with
www.architectuurgids.nl.

Editors
Paul Groenendijk, Piet Vollaard, Peter de Winter

Editing, texts and image editing
Paul Groenendijk, Peter de Winter

Translation
Jean Tee

Text editing
Leo Reijnen

Design
Koehorst in 't Veld, Bureau Sporken

Photography
Ossip van Duivenbode

Additional illustrations
Aerophotostock p.123t, Roos Aldershoff p.67b, Arnest Boender (Wiederhall 5) p.71b, Broekbakema p.123b, Buitenkunst Amsterdam p.25b, Jan Derwig p.67t, 87b, Peter Dicampos p.27b, Paul Groenendijk p.4b, 7b, 24b, 43b, i10 p.16b, KLM p.66, 80t, 111t, Job Koelewijn p.65b, John Körmeling p.36b, MVRDV p.68b, Nationaal Archief (Joost Evers) p.118b, Nationaal Archief (Roland Gerrits) p.94b, Nationaal Archief (Eric Koch) p.76b, Nationaal Archief (Ben Merk) p.81b, Nationaal Archief (Jac. de Nijs) p.100b, Nationaal Archief p.13b, 53b, 83b, Neutelings Riedijk p.96b, NOS p.119b, Office for Metropolitan Architecture p.31b, Rijksarchief voor de Nederlandse architectuur p.15b, 54b, Rijksdienst voor het Cultureel Erfgoed (Kris Roderburg, A.J. van der Wal) p.14, Rijksdienst voor het Cultureel Erfgoed (A.J. van der Wal) p.51, Rijksmuseum p.21, 34b, Piet Rook p.26b, 68t, 79t, 93m, Stadsarchief Amsterdam (Martin Alberts) p.23b, 24t, 99b, 106b, 120t, 121b, Stadsarchief Amsterdam (Jusopo Muhamad Arsath Ro'is) p.69b, 84b, Stadsarchief Amsterdam (Jan Galman) p.41b, Stadsarchief Amsterdam (Han van Gool) p.74b, Stadsarchief Amsterdam (Doriann Kransberg) p.40b, 46b, Stadsarchief Amsterdam (Jan Peeterse) p.12b, Stadsarchief Amsterdam (Freerk de Vos) p.112b, Stadsarchief Amsterdam p.9b, 10b, 11b, 20, 32, 33, 42b, 48b, 50b, 56, 57, 59b, 60b, 75b, 77b, 78b, 80b, 89b, 97b, 98b, 101b, 103, 124b, Superstudio p.107b, Veganamsterdam.org p.44b, Wikimedia p.64b, 85b, 113b, Office Winhov p.104b, Peter de Winter p.7t, 10t, 17b, 35t, 35b, 38m, 91, 95b, 125t

Printing
Wilco

Publisher
Marcel Witvoet,
nai010 publishers,
Rotterdam

ISBN 978-94-6208-841-2

NUR 648
BISAC ARC024000

Also available in a
Dutch edition
ISBN 978-94-6208-840-5

Printed and bound in
the Netherlands

© 2024 nai010 publishers, the authors, Rotterdam.

All rights reserved. No part of this publication may be reproduced, stored in a retrieval system, or transmitted in any form or by any means, electronic, mechanical, photocopying, recording or otherwise, without the prior written permission of the publisher.

For works of visual artists affiliated with a CISAC-organization the copyrights have been settled with Pictoright in Amsterdam. © 2024, c/o Pictoright Amsterdam

Although every effort was made to find the copyright holders for the illustrations used, it has not been possible to trace them all. Interested parties are requested to contact nai010 publishers, Korte Hoogstraat 31, 3011 GK Rotterdam, the Netherlands.

nai010 publishers is an internationally orientated publisher specialized in developing, producing and distributing books in the fields of architecture, urbanism, art and design. www.nai010.com

nai010 books are available internationally at selected bookstores and from the following distribution partners:

North, Central and South America - Artbook I D.A.P., New York, USA, dap@dapinc.com

Rest of the world - Idea Books, Amsterdam, the Netherlands, idea@ideabooks.nl

For general questions, please contact nai010 publishers directly at sales@nai010.com or visit our website www.nai010.com for further information.